ARROYO CENTER

Innovative Leader Development

Evaluation of the U.S. Army Asymmetric Warfare Adaptive Leader Program

Susan G. Straus, Michael G. Shanley, Carra S. Sims, Bryan W. Hallmark, Anna Rosefsky Saavedra, Stoney Trent, Sean Duggan

Prepared for the United States Army

Approved for public release; distribution unlimited

For more information on this publication, visit www.rand.org/t/rr504

Library of Congress Control Number: 2014955003

ISBN 978-0-8330-8749-2

Published by the RAND Corporation, Santa Monica, Calif.

© Copyright 2014 RAND Corporation

RAND® is a registered trademark.

Cover photo by Lt. Col. Sonise Lumbaca.

Support RAND

Make a tax-deductible charitable contribution at
www.rand.org/giving/contribute

www.rand.org

Preface

In this project, "Evaluation of U.S. Army Asymmetric Warfare Adaptive Leader Program (AWALP)," the U.S. Army Training and Doctrine Command (TRADOC) asked RAND Arroyo Center to systematically evaluate the effectiveness of AWALP and to design a set of instruments, tools, and protocols to foster ongoing assessment and improvement of AWALP and other courses or events that include adaptability training.

This report describes the study design and results based on the collection of data from three AWALP classes. Using a pretest–posttest study design, the evaluation addresses multiple outcomes, including improvement in attitudes toward adaptability, cognitive learning, and adaptability behaviors; reactions to the course; and application of adaptability principles once graduates return to their units. The report will be of interest to those seeking to measure adaptability and other intangible skills in institutional and unit training environments.

This research was sponsored by TRADOC and was conducted within the RAND Arroyo Center's Manpower and Training Program. RAND Arroyo Center, part of the RAND Corporation, is a federally funded research and development center sponsored by the United States Army.

The Project Unique Identification Code (PUIC) for the project that produced this document is RAN126497.

Correspondence regarding this report should be addressed to Susan Straus (sgstraus@rand.org) or Michael Shanley (mikes@rand.org). For more information on the RAND Arroyo Center, contact the Director of Operations, Marcy Agmon (telephone 310-393-0411, extension 6419; FAX 310-451-6952; e-mail Marcy_Agmon@rand.org); or visit Arroyo's website at http://www.rand.org/ard/.

Contents

Figures

Tables

Summary

Introduction

The type of operations the U.S. Army has confronted in the post–September 11, 2001, security environment has mandated increased adaptability in the service. Operational success requires leaders and organizations that can rapidly recognize changes in the environment, identify critical elements in unfamiliar situations with less-than-perfect information, and facilitate timely action to meet new requirements—all while under considerable stress. The need to develop adaptable leaders is articulated in key policy documents, including the U.S. Army Learning Concept for 2015 and the U.S. Army Training and Doctrine Command (TRADOC) strategic plan for 2013–2020, and it is an underlying principle in the Army's shift from a doctrine of "command and control" to "mission command" (TRADOC, 2011; TRADOC, undated). Joint Chief of Staff Chair GEN Martin Dempsey, in his former role as Commanding General, TRADOC, stressed the need for leaders who value a bottom-up over a top-down approach and emphasized the importance of developing teams that can anticipate and manage transitions.

As part of the Army's response to the need for an adaptive force, the Army's Asymmetric Warfare Group (AWG) implemented the Asymmetric Warfare Adaptive Leader Program (AWALP), a course designed to enhance adaptability in leaders and to promote innovative solutions in the training for and conduct of unified land operations. The primary goals of the course are to enhance adaptability in leaders, increase understanding of the need for adaptable soldiers and enablers of adaptive behavior, and develop leader ability to design training that fosters adaptability and its enablers.

This research documented here evaluated the effectiveness of AWALP and had three main objectives. The first was to provide a systematic evaluation of AWALP, addressing multiple individual and team outcomes and identifying potential areas for improvement in AWALP curriculum or delivery. A related aim was to identify facilitators and challenges to applying adaptability principles on the job to identify possible changes to the course or interventions to support graduates in implementing adaptability knowledge and skills.

The second objective was to provide a set of instruments, tools, and protocols that can be used to measure adaptability and to foster ongoing assessment and improvement in AWALP. Guided by a theoretical model, we designed and pilot tested a number of different measures of training outcomes to determine which provided the most useful data and provided a set of final materials to AWG based on these results.

A third objective was to provide materials suitable not only for evaluating AWALP but also for evaluating other courses or events that include adaptability training or training that addresses intangible skills more broadly (e.g., many aspects of teamwork and leadership skills). Thus, study results are intended to support not only AWG but TRADOC more generally.

AWALP Structure, Content, and Delivery

AWALP is a ten-day course, offered four times a year at Fort A.P. Hill, with 30 to 35 students per class. Each class is taught by a team of instructors (who are called *guides*), with a student-to-guide ratio of approximately 8:1. The course design is based on a taxonomy of adaptive performance (Pulakos et al., 2000) that identified eight dimensions of adaptable performance, such as solving problems creatively, dealing with changing or ambiguous situations, interpersonal adaptability, and cultural adaptability. The course consists of about 25-percent classroom instruction and 75-percent practical exercises or scenarios requiring adaptable performance.

While Army training frequently focuses on standardized procedures for accomplishing tasks, AWALP uses an outcomes-based
approach, focusing more on the results the commander intends to
achieve. Although how tasks are executed is still important, achieving
the results is considered to be more important than the actions used
to attain the results (as long as the actions do not violate the commander's intent). This approach encourages trainees to take initiative
and adjust their actions to adapt to the situation, which require independent thinking and problem solving. After a training event, guides
facilitate an after-action review (AAR) that promotes self-discovery of
lessons learned. These training processes promote accountability and
foster an understanding not only of what needs to be done but why
certain actions are required—principles that are aligned clearly with
the doctrine of mission command.

Research Design

We addressed individual, team, and leadership aspects of adaptability while addressing significant challenges to measuring adaptability.
These challenges include the need to measure intangible concepts, the
response burden that a comprehensive analysis can impose, and a lack
of established measures of adaptability. We used several strategies to
address these challenges. First, we used multiple approaches to measuring adaptability, including piloting new ones, to assess a range of
adaptability training outcomes and to offset the weaknesses of any one
method or measure with other approaches. Second, for most outcome
measures, we used a pretest–posttest design and included measures of
individual differences associated with adaptive performance. In contrast to posttest-only designs that are typically used in training evaluation, this approach enabled us to assess the impact of AWALP training. Third, we balanced the comprehensiveness of the approach with
response burden by focusing the evaluation on the factors most critical
to adaptability and to the levels of adaptability addressed in AWALP.

The evaluation included assessment of outcomes reflecting different goals of training. These included

- *reactions* to the course—satisfaction with course content, design, and delivery
- *attitudes* and *learning*—how training results in changes in learners
- *transfer performance and results*—how training brings about pay-offs to the organization.

We also measured individual factors that influence or point to reasons for training outcomes. Including these measures can improve the ability to predict or explain training outcomes and can enable designers and instructors to modify aspects of the course, such as prerequisites, curriculum, or delivery, to improve outcomes. We measured individual characteristics most relevant to training outcomes in AWALP, such as Big Five personality traits, general cognitive ability, learning goal orientation, and various demographic characteristics.

The evaluation was based on data from 104 students enrolled in three AWALP classes in 2013.

Results

Reaction to AWALP

Students were extremely satisfied with the course structure, content, and delivery. AWALP students attribute their learning largely to the content of the course and the training methods, which differ substantially from typical Army training. All AWALP students reported that they would recommend the course to others, largely because of the course concepts, the training approach, and improved cognition. In addition, interviews of course graduates three months following AWALP showed that reactions remained favorable over time. Overall, we found that students' reactions to AWALP were much more favorable than active-duty leaders' attitudes about institutional training in general, as reported in the 2013 Center for Army Leadership Annual Survey of Army Leadership (CASAL) survey.

Students anticipated that leader buy-in and command climate would pose challenges to applying adaptability concepts on

the job. Leader buy-in was mentioned most often, by nearly one-third of the students. Command climate was the second most frequently anticipated barrier, reported by 20 percent of the students. Despite these expected challenges, almost one-third of the students expressed a sense of determination to overcome these challenges.

Attitudes Toward Adaptability

Pretraining and posttraining surveys measured three types of attitudes toward the dimensions of adaptive performance: self-efficacy, interest in being adaptable, and the frequency with which students engage in relevant behaviors on their jobs (pretest) or should do so (posttest). The surveys asked the same kinds of attitude questions for behaviors pertaining to putting adaptability into leader practice, such as coaching others, seeking subordinate input, and seeking consensus on decisions. Results show improvement in almost all aspects of attitudes toward adaptability. After the course, students thought they were better at being adaptable in all dimensions and in leader practice (see Figure S.1). They also reported greater interest in adaptability than before the course.

Results show substantial improvement in self-efficacy and interest, even after accounting for students' individual differences that are associated with adaptability. Students' self-efficacy and interest for all dimensions of adaptability and leader practice increased and were rated highly following AWALP, regardless of individual characteristics, such as openness to experience, conscientiousness, extraversion, learning and performance orientations, motivation for training, and time in service.

Results also suggest an increase in the perceived need for adaptability and adaptive leader behaviors in the students' current jobs. At the end of the course, students saw their jobs as requiring greater adaptive performance with respect to all the dimensions of adaptability and the majority of leader behaviors assessed. **Thus, after the course, students not only sensed a change in their own capabilities and interests about adaptability but appeared to see their work contexts in a different light.**

Figure S.1
Self-Efficacy Ratings Pre- and Posttraining

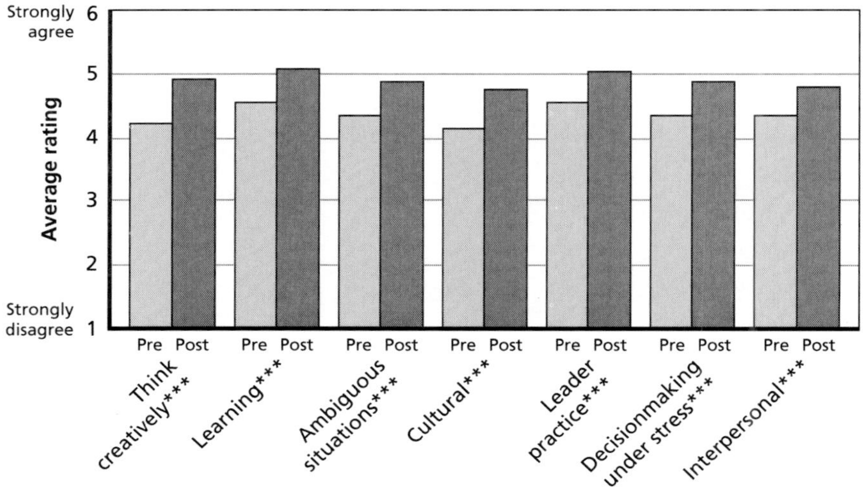

NOTE: ***$p < 0.001$.

RAND *RR504-S.1*

Knowledge of Course Concepts

Students demonstrated increased knowledge of AWALP concepts.
Average scores on a multiple-choice knowledge test were 60 percent correct pretraining and 76 percent correct posttraining. As with results for self-efficacy and interest in adaptability, students showed improved knowledge regardless of other characteristics associated with test performance, including general cognitive ability and level of education. **These results indicate that AWALP was successful at fostering knowledge gain for a wide range of students.**

Team Performance

We developed a measure to assess adaptability at the team level for practical exercises, using both the students and guides as raters of team adaptive performance. The measure required raters to assess whether the dimensions of adaptive performance were required in each exercise and to rate the team's effectiveness on these dimensions. Participants were asked to complete the rating form after team exercises on days 3, 5, and 7.

The similarity between students' and guides' ratings of adaptability requirements varied across the three exercises. For example, students failed to recognize that some adaptability dimensions were not relevant, particularly in the first two exercises. However, results also indicate that students were starting to discriminate between dimensions of adaptability that were and were not required by the third exercise. The number of and degree of discrepancies between students' and guides' ratings also decreased over time, suggesting that students were becoming more accurate in their ratings of requirements.

Figure S.2 shows effectiveness ratings aggregated across the three exercises. **In general, both students and guides gave favorable ratings of team performance.** Students' average scores hovered around 5, corresponding to an "agree" response, and most of the guides' ratings ranged from approximately 4 (i.e., agree somewhat) to 5 (Figure S.2). **However, students consistently gave higher ratings of team performance than guides did.** As might be expected given the differences

Figure S.2
Student and Guide Ratings of Team Effectiveness Aggregated Across Exercises

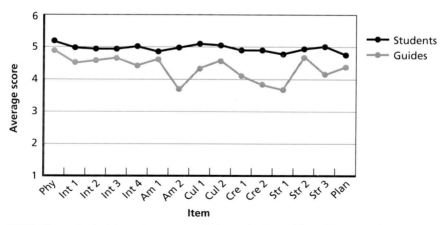

NOTE: Phy = physical, Int = interpersonal, Am = dealing with ambiguity, Cul = cultural, Str = decisionmaking under stress, Plan = planning.

in their experience levels, **students also generally discriminated less than guides did in rating team performance across the different dimensions of adaptability.** As shown in Figure S.2, students' ratings of team performance were more similar across the items, as indicated by the relatively flatter slope for their ratings.

At the same time, students also perceived that team effectiveness was increasing, a view that guides did not necessarily share. In the first two exercises, students rated their teams higher on some dimensions, and guides rated teams higher on others. However, in the third exercise, students rated their teams higher than guides did on *all* the items. **Thus, students' ratings of effectiveness changed over time, but they appeared to become more confident about the level of adaptability in their teams as the course progressed.**

Application of AWALP Principles on the Job

We conducted telephone interviews of students and their supervisors at three and six months postgraduation to assess the longer-term impact of AWALP on adaptability behavior and attitudes after students returned to their units. In interviews conducted three months after AWALP, graduates reported substantial application of AWALP principles on the job, especially in the areas of coaching, training, delegating to subordinates, and seeking subordinate input. Moreover, many graduates reported applying outcomes-based strategies for these activities, giving more freedom to subordinates to address tasks and challenges. For most, these positive effects of AWALP were sustained six months after graduation. Changes were less common in other areas, such as conducting AARs and briefing commanding officers, largely because many of the graduates reported no opportunity to engage in these activities in their current roles. While AWALP principles were successfully disseminated to graduates' subordinates, dissemination was somewhat less successful to peers and commanders and throughout the unit.

Graduates also remained extremely positive about AWALP three months after the course. All graduates reported that they would still recommend the course to others, and few recommended course changes. However, graduates also saw the same obstacles to applying

AWALP principles once back at their units, with command climate and entrenched leadership still the most frequently mentioned challenges.

Supervisors were also positive about the effect of AWALP on graduates' behavior, particularly with respect to observing improvements in training planning and communications with the commanding officers. However, results should be interpreted with caution, because the sample size of supervisors was extremely small. Difficulties in recruiting supervisors for interviews were likely partly because the evaluation was a research study and therefore required graduates' consent to contact their supervisors. We recommend several strategies for recruiting supervisors in future evaluation efforts.

Summary, Conclusions, and Future Directions

The results of this evaluation provide evidence of AWALP's success across a range of measures, including reactions to the course, changes in learner attitudes and cognitive learning, and recognition of the need for adaptability in situations encountered on the job.

Recommendations to Improve AWALP

Students had few recommendations for improving AWALP, and other study results showed limited need for modifications to the course.

One recommendation is to put more emphasis on anticipating and responding to potential challenges to implementing AWALP principles on the job. At the end of the course, students expected that leader buy-in and command climate would pose the greatest obstacles to implementation, and interviews with graduates three and six months after the course confirmed that these factors indeed presented obstacles. Over time, we expect that receptivity to adaptability concepts will improve as a critical mass of soldiers participates in the course or learns about adaptability in other Army training. In the meantime, however, we recommend explicitly discussing in AWALP these potential obstacles and strategies to address them.

Second, although students generally were satisfied with the feedback guides provided, use of the team rating instrument within an

AAR could further enhance feedback and might foster student self-awareness and convergence of students' and guides' ratings, which remained discrepant on day 7 of the course. Student ratings could be useful in several ways; for example, student ratings could point to topics that are particularly important for guides to probe in the AAR, and asking students to complete the team rating form before and after the AAR (rather than just before) might encourage them to reflect more deeply on their performance. Guides' ratings of students' individual effectiveness could be another source of feedback. We discuss this topic below.

Third, while AWALP already addresses important team behaviors, model development since the inception of the course has advanced theory of team adaptability and related outcomes. The curriculum could be enhanced by reinforcing important team-level concepts (e.g., mutual monitoring and backup behavior) and by providing instruction about the relationships among inputs to the team, throughputs, and outcomes.

Fourth, variation in students' responses across different measures used in the evaluation and/or discrepancies between students' assessments and guides' evaluations suggest that instruction could be enhanced for some adaptability dimensions. These include handling ambiguous situations, generating innovative ideas, and cultural adaptability.

Finally, a related topic for AWG consideration is whether students' posttraining knowledge test scores are acceptable. If they are not satisfactory, additional reinforcement of course concepts in classroom instruction and during practical exercises may be needed. Likewise, if scores on ratings of team performance are not satisfactory, additional strategies may be needed to enable students to demonstrate improved adaptability in team contexts.

Recommended Measures and Processes for Ongoing Evaluation

We recommend that AWG continue to administer several of the instruments used in this evaluation, including the knowledge test, questions about attitudes toward adaptability and leader practice, reactions to the course, and ratings of team adaptive performance. We propose a number of revisions to these measures to reduce the response burden and to better capture important aspects of team collaboration and performance, such as planning, mutual monitoring, and backup behavior. We also recommend administering the instruments online rather than using paper and pencils to improve the efficiency and accuracy of data collection, allow responses to be scored immediately, and allow the collection of additional information about the quality of students' responses.

We also recommend continuing to assess how graduates apply AWALP principles on the job through interviews of course graduates. As another indicator of success, we recommend tracking multiple enrollments from the same units over time. In addition, a number of different Army divisions have asked AWG for support in standing up local adaptability training modeled after AWALP. These requests can serve as additional indicators of AWALP success.

Recommendations for Future Evaluation of AWALP

Additional methods and measures can contribute to a more comprehensive evaluation of AWALP. A theme of many of these recommendations is the need to obtain additional measures of adaptive performance. Some suggestions are as follows:

- Most important is assessing transfer of training by assessing the association of individual characteristics and outcomes measured in training with the quality of subsequent job performance. To accomplish this, we propose that guides rate student performance in AWALP and that graduates' supervisors provide independent, quantifiable ratings of subsequent job performance. For greater success in contacting supervisors, we recommend modifying the recruiting processes used in the current study. Specific recommendations include obtaining supervisor contact information on student enrollment in AWALP, contacting supervisors after three months rather than after a longer time interval, and giving priority for future AWALP enrollments to supervisors who provide feedback about course graduates.

- Assessing transfer of training could be expanded further by collecting feedback from not only graduates' supervisors but also from graduates' peers and subordinates. Assessment could be strengthened by including a matched sample of leaders who have not attended AWALP. The Army's Multi-Source Assessment and Feedback Program, a 360-degree evaluation process for officers, could serve as a model for this effort.
- More-extensive behavioral observations of individuals or teams could be used to obtain additional measures of effectiveness in AWALP and to assess improvement in performance as the course progresses. For example, guides could use behavior checklists to rate the frequency of adaptability behaviors exhibited in parallel practical exercises conducted at the beginning and end of the course (e.g., Roselle, 2013). As mentioned above, ratings of individuals would also provide predictor measures for studying training transfer.

Expanding AWALP's Approach to Adaptability Training

The Army should consider ways to leverage AWG's approach by incorporating AWALP principles into other Army training. One strategy is to increase the number of trainees in the existing course or modified versions of it. For example, AWG could continue to support standing up AWALP training in Army divisions by training local trainers or through mobile training teams. Another way to disseminate AWALP more broadly is to incorporate adaptability principles into existing professional military education courses required for promotion, such as advanced leader courses, senior leader courses, the Basic Officer Leader Course, Captains' Career Course, and intermediate-level education.

TRADOC can also support mission command principles by expanding on instruction of team adaptability. AWALP provides a starting point for training soldiers to work in and lead teams, but there are many additional topics that foster effective teams and effective team leaders. Given the large and growing literature relevant to team adaptability, we recommend developing an AWALP follow-on course focused exclusively on these topics. Alternatively, some existing leader-development institutional courses or other training that focuses on team interaction and performance might also provide an appropriate context for this training. Examples of prospective team-based training topics include shared mental models, transactive memory systems, team trust, process losses in group tasks, and team facilitation.

To support expansion of AWG's approach to adaptability training, we recommend that AWG create a training support package for AWALP with a program of instruction and supplementary materials. While a conventional Army program of instruction may not be appropriate for AWALP in light of its teaching approach, a set of organized materials will help preserve institutional knowledge related to training adaptability and will support dissemination of course content and instructional methods to the Army at large.

Lessons for Adaptability Evaluation in Other Training Contexts

Lessons learned from this research apply to measuring adaptability and other intangible concepts not only in AWALP but also in other training contexts. The evaluation demonstrates the benefits of using multiple measures and methods and documents how such measures can be developed and implemented to assess intangible training outcomes. Evaluations of other courses that involve adaptability training can make use of most of the reactions measures implemented in this study "as is" or with minor modifications. Pre-post knowledge tests, attitudinal measures, and postgraduate interviews can be used with appropriate revisions for course content. Instructor and student ratings of team performance may be broadly applicable to Army training. Continued use of these instruments, including the modifications suggested above and described in more detail in this report, can provide data to validate the measures and support TRADOC in evaluating a wide range of training efforts that emphasize 21st-century soldier skills.

Conclusion

The shift in Army doctrine from command and control to mission command calls for profound changes in leader and team conduct. These changes in philosophy require a concomitant transformation in training. AWG's successful development and implementation of AWALP exemplifies mission command principles in terms of both the content of the course and the manner in which it is taught. AWALP, supported by systematic course evaluation, provides a promising approach for the Army as it seeks to further develop adaptable leaders and teams.

Acknowledgments

This research would not have been possible without the assistance of many people in AWG. We are especially grateful to LTC (ret.) Blaise "CD" Cornell-d'Echert, Jr., and SGM (ret.) Wayne Newberry for sharing their time, expertise, and effort throughout all phases of the study, from writing test items to advising on development of other instruments, providing course materials, handling the logistics of our visits, responding to our many email messages and phone calls, and generally demonstrating adaptability to ensure that we could conduct this research. We wish to acknowledge CSM (ret.) Hugh Roberts and the entire cadre of AWALP guides for their contributions and assistance in instrument development and in supporting the study more generally. We also thank LTC Michael McCay and other AWG leadership for their contributions and support throughout this project. Finally, we wish to thank the AWALP students for their efforts in filling out our surveys, sometimes after long training days.

Several members of our RAND team also provided invaluable help on this research. We especially wish to thank Jeremy Miles, Claude Messan Setodji, and Michael Robbins for their assistance with data analysis and to Caroline Epley for her role in data collection. We wish to acknowledge Paul Steinberg for his incisive revisions to this report and Phyllis Gilmore for her meticulous editing.

Many thanks to Sean Robson from RAND and Eduardo Salas from University of Central Florida for their thoughtful and insightful reviews of this report.

Abbreviations

AAR	after-action review
ADP	Army Doctrine Publication
Am	dealing with ambiguity
ATOM	Anti-Air Teamwork Observation Measure
AWALP	Asymmetric Warfare Adaptive Leader Program
AWG	Asymmetric Warfare Group
CASAL	Center for Army Leadership Annual Survey of Army Leadership
Cre	creative thinking
Cul	cultural
FFI	Five-Factor Inventory
ICC	intraclass correlation
Int	interpersonal
NCO	noncommissioned officer
OBT&E	outcomes-based training and education
Phy	physical
Plan	planning

PME   professional military education

POI   program of instruction

PT   physical training

Str   decisionmaking under stress

TRADOC   Training and Doctrine Command

CHAPTER ONE

Introduction

Background

The Need for Adaptability

The type of operations the U.S. Army has confronted in the post–September 11, 2001, security environment has shown the need for increased adaptability in the service. For example, as Burke, Pierce, and Salas, 2006, p. ix, notes:

> The US military is facing an increasingly complex geopolitical environment that also demands adaptability in order to be effective. For example, within the military, individuals are having to adapt to asymmetric threats, increased joint operations, and network capabilities. Teams are having to adapt to a wide variety of environmental and team composition factors (e.g., warfighting, peacekeeping, teams comprised of coalition partners of multiple nationalities), and at the organizational level the military is having to adapt to changes in the geopolitical environment.

The Army must develop soldiers prepared for operations in an environment that is complex, ambiguous, and highly uncertain and in one that demands action within shorter time frames (Zaccaro et al., 2009). Operational success will require leaders and organizations that can rapidly adapt by recognizing changes in the environment, identifying critical elements of the new situation with less-than-perfect information, and facilitating timely action to meet new requirements—all while under considerable stress.

Senior Army leaders have emphasized the importance of developing a more-adaptive force and have identified "adaptability and initiative" as key 21st-century soldier competencies (U.S. Training and Doctrine Command [TRADOC], 2011). According to Army Chief of Staff GEN Ray Odierno, developing adaptive leaders is a top priority for the Army (38th Army Chief of Staff, 2013). Joint Chief of Staff Chair GEN Martin Dempsey, in his former role as Commanding General, TRADOC, emphasized the need to seek and embrace adaptability to confront hybrid threats. In describing a shift from a doctrine of "command and control" to "mission command," General Dempsey also stressed the need for teams that can anticipate and manage transitions and leaders who value a bottom-up over a top-down approach and who "pass resources and responsibility 'to the edge'" (Dempsey, 2011, p. 44). The exercise of mission command, as described in Army Doctrine Publication (ADP) 6-0, 2012, p. 1, calls for commanders to "empower agile and adaptive leaders" guided by principles that include building cohesive teams through mutual trust, creating shared understanding, and exercising disciplined initiative. Likewise, in TRADOC's strategic plan for 2013–2020, Commanding General of TRADOC, GEN Robert Cone, emphasized the need to train leaders to be adaptable (TRADOC, undated).

As part of the Army's response to the need for an adaptive force, the Army's Asymmetric Warfare Group (AWG) implemented the Asymmetric Warfare Adaptive Leader Program (AWALP) in 2011, a course designed to enhance adaptability in leaders and to promote innovative solutions in training and unified land operations. AWG, in turn, asked RAND Arroyo Center to conduct an evaluation of the effectiveness of AWALP. This document represents the final report on that evaluation.

Definition and Dimensions of Adaptability

AWG's definition of adaptability, which we also use, comes from Army Field Manual 6-22, 2006. The shorter version of that definition, which is used in AWALP training materials, defines adaptability as "an effective change in behavior in response to an altered situation." An expanded version, also cited in AWG's leaders guide, emphasizes the individual's role in bringing about the needed change: "Adaptability is an individual's ability to recognize change in the environment, identify the critical elements of the new situation, and trigger changes accordingly to meet new requirements."

The conceptual basis for AWALP design comes from the Pulakos et al., 2000, model of adaptive performance. Pulakos et al., 2000, presents and tests a taxonomy positing eight dimensions of adaptive performance (Figure 1.1).[1] (See Chapter Two for a description of how the taxonomy was developed and tested.) AWG staff adopted the Pulakos et al. taxonomy for several reasons: It is well-documented, and its focus on observable behaviors of the adaptive performance dimensions supported the design of course activities; the research used to establish the dimensions included a large number of military respondents, which contributed to buy-in among Army stakeholders; and U.S. Army Research Institute research documented application of

Figure 1.1
The Eight Dimensions of Adaptability

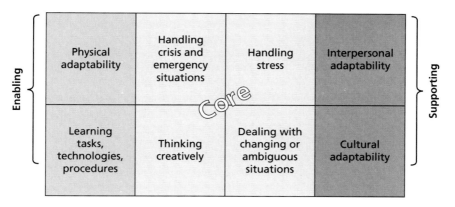

NOTE: The original eight dimensions are from Pulakos et al., 2000. AWG developed the additional categorizations (enabling, core, and supporting) for AWALP.
RAND RR504-1.1

---

[1] Some researchers distinguish between the terms *adaptation* and *adaptability*, with the former referring to performance and the latter to an individual characteristic (e.g., see Baard, Rench, and Kozlowski, 2014). However, AWG and this report use these terms interchangeably.

the model in an adaptive thinking and leadership course for Special Forces officer candidates (White et al., 2005) and found additional support for the model (Tucker and Gunther, 2009; Zaccaro et al., 2009). Although there is some evidence that there may be a simpler structure with fewer than eight dimensions of adaptive performance (e.g., Griffin and Hesketh, 2003; Pulakos et al., 2002), Baard, Rench, and Kozlowski, 2014, recommend using the Pulakos et al., 2000, taxonomy as a starting point for research in light of its rigorous theoretical and empirical foundations, coupled with a lack of theory and systematic research in alternative formulations of adaptive performance (and indeed, the Pulakos et al., 2000, taxonomy has been very influential in other theoretical perspectives, e.g., Ployhart and Bliese, 2006).[2]

In AWALP, four of the eight adaptive performance dimensions (shown in the middle of Figure 1.1) are considered to be core, two dimensions are considered to be enabling, and two are considered to be supporting.[3] The dimensions are defined in Table 1.1.[4]

AWALP Structure and Content

AWALP is a ten-day course for noncommissioned officers (NCOs) and junior officers primarily in the active component. It began in 2011 and is currently taught four times a year in residence at Fort A.P. Hill to about 30 to 35 students per class. Each class is taught by a team of instructors, called *guides*, which reflects their primary role as facilitators rather than teachers. The guides initially selected for the course were highly experienced, retired special operations forces operators with a demonstrated proficiency in teaching marksmanship and tactical problem solving and who supported the guiding principles of the

---

[2]   For example, Entin and Serfaty, 1999, found a three-factor solution of proactive behaviors, such as thinking creatively; reactive behaviors, such as interpersonal and cultural adaptability; and tolerant behaviors, such as handling stress. The overlap with the Pulakos et al., 2000, taxonomy is evident.

[3]   AWG further organized the dimensions into three larger categories: physical (physical adaptability), interpersonal (interpersonal adaptability and cultural adaptability), and cognitive (the four core dimensions in Figure 1.1, plus "learning tasks, technologies, procedures.")

[4]   The definitions are based on those in Asymmetric Warfare Adaptive Leader Program, *Leader's Guide for Enhancing Adaptability*, December 2011, pp. 4–5.

Table 1.1
Definitions of Adaptability Dimensions

Dimension	Definition
Thinking creatively	Developing innovative solutions to problems by entertaining a wide range of options, developing innovative methods of achieving outcomes with limited resources, and integrating seemingly unconnected information into logical patterns that increase situational awareness
Dealing with changing or ambiguous situations	Using critical thinking to define the nature of a problem; taking effective action when needed, even without all desired information; and responding to changing environments with cognitive flexibility
Learning work tasks, technologies, and procedures	Taking action to improve work performance through a process of self-reflection
	By taking action, learning new skills or gaining information in response to an altered situation or preparing for future possibilities
Interpersonal adaptability	Participating and working well with others as a team member and building positive, effective relationships, including listening to and understanding others
	Learning how to effectively lead a discussion
Cultural adaptability	Communicating effectively across a diversity of cultures, regardless of differences
	Being willing to adjust behavior to comply with or show respect for others' values and customs
Decisionmaking under stress	Remaining resilient and taking appropriate actions when confronted by various stressors
	Being a calming influence on others
Handling emergencies and crises	Reacting effectively in life-threatening situations (e.g., staying clear and focused and making swift decisions)
	Having ability to apply emergency techniques and skills when accidents or injuries occur
Physical adaptability	Having or training to obtain the weight, strength, and endurance necessary for your job and to go beyond it
	Adjusting oneself to complete demanding tasks and to operate in varied environments and under austere conditions

NOTE: AWG's terms for some of the dimensions are slightly different from those of Pulakos et al., 2000. Pulakos et al. used "Solving problems creatively" rather than "Thinking creatively" and used "Dealing with uncertain and unpredictable work situations" rather than "Dealing with changing or ambiguous situations." These variations in terminology do not affect the substantive focus of the dimensions. However, while Pulakos et al., 2000, identified a dimension entitled "Handling work stress," AWALP focuses specifically on "decisionmaking under stress."

course. Later guides were selected to have the same or similar skills and attitudes. The student-to-guide ratio is approximately 8:1. The course is unlike most Army institutional training in that it does not have a formal program of instruction (POI) with enabling or terminal learning objectives. The primary goals of the course are to enhance adaptability in leaders, increase understanding of the need for adaptable soldiers and enablers of adaptive behavior,[5] and develop leader ability to design training that fosters adaptability and its enablers.

The course presents a variety of learning experiences, consisting of about 75 percent hands-on activities and 25 percent classroom instruction. The course seeks to fundamentally transform students' thinking about what it means to be a leader and trainer and how to get the most out of the teams they lead. The first phase of the course (approximately the first five days) uses classroom activities and focused practical field exercises to develop individual and team adaptability. This phase is devoted to ensuring that participants understand the dimensions of adaptive performance, how adaptability fosters individual and team performance, and how that performance leads to the agility and operational adaptability needed for current operations. The second phase presents more-complex problems reflecting contemporary operational challenges. This phase is intended to help students learn to respond to asymmetric threats in different operational environments. The second phase also places special emphasis on developing leaders' abilities to design unit training that integrates adaptability concepts.

The course does not cover each of the dimensions of adaptive performance shown in Table 1.1 to an equal degree. Creative thinking; dealing with ambiguity; learning tasks, technologies, and procedures; interpersonal adaptability; and handling stress are embedded into nearly all course events. Cultural adaptability is represented somewhat less. The course puts little emphasis on physical adaptability because the terrain at the training site is not conducive to conducting practical

---

[5]   While two of the dimensions are considered enabling, the term *enabler* here refers to other factors that foster adaptive behavior. These include opportunities for trainees to test their confidence, practice decisionmaking, practice innovative problem solving, and demonstrate initiative, all with an awareness of accountability.

exercises that test this dimension. Likewise, the course does not address responding to crisis situations because it lacks appropriate training facilities to create high-fidelity crisis scenarios.

The curriculum is highly experiential. Each day, students complete one or more practical exercises that are designed to tap a subset of the adaptive performance dimensions (see Appendix A for an exemplar exercise). Some of the exercises create realistic, simulated military scenarios (as described in Chapter Four), while others consist of more-general problem-solving activities (e.g., puzzles, tower building). Instructional practices largely reflect constructivist educational principles, many of which are also consistent with recommended strategies for training for team adaptation (see Burke, Stagl, et al., 2006). Common constructivist strategies include (Gagne et al., 2005):

- working in collaborative groups
- presenting novel problems to solve in realistic settings (called *situated learning* or *problem-based learning*; e.g., Anderson, Reder and Simon, 1996; Lave and Wenger, 1991; Savery and Duffy, 1995).
- challenging students with tasks just beyond their current skill level to motivate them and build their confidence
- providing opportunities for practice in similar situations
- providing guidance from instructors prepared to intervene as needed (called *guided discovery*)
- encouraging students to reflect on the learning process and their skill acquisition.

In addition, while much of Army training frequently focuses on learning standardized procedures to accomplish tasks, AWALP uses an outcomes-based approach, focusing more on the results the commander hopes to achieve.[6] Although how tasks are executed is still important, achieving the results is considered to be more important

---

[6] This approach is referred to as *outcomes-based training and education* (OBT&E). OBT&E concepts were developed in the Army (see Haskins, 2010) and are similar to ideas of outcomes-based education as discussed by William Spady (Cornell-d'Echert, personal communication, November 12, 2013). While OBT&E concepts are similar to some established theories in organizational behavior, such as goal setting, we have not been able to find empirical research investigating OBT&E.

than the actions used to attain the outcomes (as long as the actions do not violate the commander's intent). Consistent with constructivism, this gives trainees the freedom to take initiative, adjust their actions, and adapt to the situation, which require them to engage in independent thinking and problem solving. After a training event, the instructor facilitates an after-action review (AAR) that promotes self-discovery of lessons learned. These training processes promote accountability and an understanding not only of *what* needs to be done but *why* certain actions are required, which, in turn, is thought to empower trainees and foster their confidence. These instructional strategies are aligned clearly with the principles of mission command. According to ADP 6-0, 2012, to support decisionmaking at the point of action, commanders must

> concentrate on the objectives of an operation, not how to achieve it. Commanders provide subordinates with their intent, the purpose of the operation, the key tasks, the desired end state, and resources. Subordinates then exercise disciplined initiative to respond to unanticipated problems.

Objectives

In response to AWG's request, we designed and conducted an evaluation of AWALP to achieve three main objectives.[7] The first was to systematically evaluate the effectiveness of AWALP, addressing multiple individual and team outcomes. The evaluation focused on four primary customers: AWALP program designers, guides (i.e., instructors), course graduates, and TRADOC. One evaluation focus was on identifying potential areas for improvement in AWALP itself, either in the curriculum or in how it is taught, by measuring training outcomes

---

[7] At the time that we began our research, AWG was engaged in a study examining changes in attitudes toward adaptability and adaptable performance from the beginning to the end of the course, along with interviews of graduates to assess their views of the course and how it had affected their jobs (Roselle, 2013). Because this study was in progress, results were not available to inform the design of our evaluation; however, we have integrated the findings into our report where appropriate.

during and immediately following the course. A related aim was to identify facilitators and challenges to applying adaptability principles on the job, with the goal of using the results to suggest additional changes in the course content or interventions to support graduates in implementing adaptability concepts once they return to their jobs.

The second study objective was to provide a set of instruments, tools, and protocols that could be used to measure adaptive performance and to foster ongoing assessment and improvement in AWALP. Guided by a theoretical model of training evaluation and effectiveness, we designed and pilot tested a number of different measures to determine which provided the most useful data. Final materials differ somewhat from those used during the project because our evaluation included efforts to minimize response burden and to simplify administration and analyses required on an ongoing basis.

A third study objective was to provide materials suitable not only for evaluating AWALP but for evaluating other courses or events that include adaptability training or training that addresses intangible skills more broadly (e.g., many aspects of teamwork and leadership skills). Thus, study results are intended to support not only AWG but TRADOC more generally.

Organization of This Report

Chapter Two presents a brief review of adaptability from the research literature and describes our study design, which is driven by that review.

We present more-detailed descriptions of the methods and analyses and results from our evaluation in the three subsequent chapters. Chapter Three addresses students' reactions and attitudes, and Chapter Four addresses student learning. Chapter Five describes graduates' application of AWALP principles on the job and graduates' attitudes toward AWALP after returning to their units.

Chapter Six summarizes our findings and conclusions and presents recommendations for revising the course, for ongoing evaluation of AWALP, and for future evaluation of AWALP and related courses.

Finally, a series of appendixes provides supplementary information.

CHAPTER TWO

General Approach and Study Design

We begin with an overview of the general approach that guided our study design, particularly in selecting training evaluation and effectiveness measures. This includes a brief review of findings from the research literature that bear on the content of the measures and a description of general challenges in measuring adaptability. We then discuss our study design and how the design addresses the challenges.

General Approach

Underlying Model of Training Evaluation and Effectiveness

Our evaluation design was guided by a model of training evaluation and effectiveness adapted from Alvarez, Salas, and Garofano, 2004, which we have used in prior research (Straus, Shanley, Lytell, et al., 2013; Straus, Shanley, Yeung, et al., 2011; see the last report for a detailed description of the model). The model identifies outcome measures to evaluate training and factors that may influence or explain these outcomes. Outcome measures indicate whether a course meets its intended goals (e.g., whether students learn the material or apply trained skills on the job). Alvarez, Salas, and Garofano, 2004, identifies five types of outcome measures based on the four-level classification system (reactions, learning, behavior or on-the-job performance, and results) in Kirkpatrick, 1994. The outcomes reflect different aspects or goals of training:

- *Reactions* address training content and design (and we would argue, delivery).
- *Affective outcomes (i.e., attitudes)* and *learning* address how training results in changes in learners.
- *Transfer performance* and *results* address how training brings about payoffs to the organization.

Explanatory factors influence or point to reasons for training outcomes (e.g., students with low levels of experience do not benefit from training as much as students with higher levels of experience; students with a "mastery" learning orientation perform better than students with a "performance" orientation).[1] Including measures of such factors can improve our ability to predict or explain adaptive performance and can enable designers and instructors to modify aspects of the course, such as prerequisites, curriculum, and delivery, to improve training outcomes.

Our evaluation of AWALP included measures of reactions, affective outcomes, learning, and application of course principles on the job as a proxy for transfer performance. The substantive focus of these measures was based on the research literature, which we discuss next.

Research Literature Relevant to Measuring AWALP Effectiveness

AWALP addresses adaptability at the individual level, at the team level, and at the intersection of the two—at the level of leadership. We briefly explore the research literature about adaptability at each of these levels and explain how the research findings informed our measures.

Individual Adaptability
Background

Although numerous authors have discussed adaptability, Pulakos and her colleagues (Pulakos, Arad, et al., 2000; Pulakos, Schmitt, et al.,

---

[1]   *Mastery* and *performance orientations* refer to motivational dispositions relevant to learning or learning goal orientations (Dweck, 1986). Individuals with a *mastery orientation* are interested in learning for the sake of learning; they seek learning and improvement. Individuals with a *performance orientation* are interested in learning primarily to perform better on tasks; they are interested primarily in demonstrating competence.

2002) are credited with synthesizing ongoing research streams under the rubric of adaptability, specifically in the service of defining adaptive performance (see Baard, Rench, and Kozlowski, 2014; Ployhart and Bliese, 2006). Pulakos, Arad, et al., 2000, built on the well-established job performance model put forward by Campbell and his colleagues that emphasizes a focus on observable behavior and that breaks performance into a multidimensional construct (Campbell, 1990; Campbell et al., 1993). Although they attempted to model the full breadth of relevant job performance, Campbell and his colleagues did not necessarily include a component in their model that covered changes in behavior to enable adaptation—adaptive performance as synthesized by Pulakos, Arad, et al., 2000.

In the Pulakos et al. taxonomy, adaptive performance is conceived of as domain general rather than as domain specific—that is, performance as relevant to a broad range of tasks (see Baard, Rench, and Kozlowski, 2014). Pulakos and her colleagues define adaptive performance as comprising eight factors, as described in Chapter One. In developing their taxonomy, they drew from the organizational literature and from an extensive database of critical performance incidents that described the situation, outcome, and conditions surrounding instances of both high and low performance in a wide range of occupations (Pulakos, Arad, et al., 2000). The design of AWALP—and the measures we used in the evaluation—are based on these dimensions of adaptive performance. In addition to identifying dimensions of adaptive performance, Pulakos, Schmitt, et al., 2002, investigated the association of potential attitudinal and experiential predictors (self-efficacy, interest, and experience measures aligned with the eight dimensions) with adaptive job performance in a study of Army personnel. Their results on finding separate dimensions in supervisors' ratings of adaptive performance of study participants were equivocal; for supervisor ratings, a single factor was found to fit the data best. However, support was found for distinctions among the eight factors for three separate types of predictor questions, i.e., participants' ratings of their interest in adaptability, self-efficacy to adapt, and experience in adapting. Moreover, experience in adapting added incrementally to predicting supervisors' ratings of adaptive performance, over and above other relevant and well-established traditional predictors of job performance (i.e., general cognitive ability and personality traits, including achievement orientation and openness to experience),[2] although experience in only one adaptability dimension (i.e., learning tasks, technologies, and procedures) was positively and significantly associated with performance ratings.[3]

More generally, there is a large body of research documenting the association of individual characteristics with job performance. Studies show consistent and positive relationships between job performance and general cognitive ability (e.g., Hunter and Hunter, 1984; LePine, Colquitt, and Erez, 2000; Ree and Earles, 1991; 1992; Ree, Earles, and Teachout, 1994; Schmidt and Hunter, 2004); learning goal orientation (e.g., Dweck, 1986; Fisher and Ford, 1998; Klein, Noe and Wang, 2006; Mesmer-Magnus and Viswesvaran, 2007; Phillips and Gully, 1997); and personality traits, such as conscientiousness, extraversion, and openness to experience (e.g., Barrick and Mount, 1991). Research also documents the association of individual characteristics with leader effectiveness. In a four-year longitudinal study of U.S. Military Academy cadets, Bartone, Snook, and Tremble, 2002, found that general intellectual abilities and two of the Big Five personality variables (agreeableness and conscientiousness) predicted leader performance.[4] Using meta-analysis, Judge and his colleagues have also found that Big Five personality characteristics predict leader performance. Judge and Bono, 2000, showed that conscientiousness and extraversion predicted transformational leadership. Judge et al., 2002, found that, of the Big Five traits, extraversion was the most consistently associated with leader emergence and leader effectiveness, followed by conscientiousness and openness to experience.

---

[2]   Note, however, that openness was negatively related to performance.

[3]   Experience in interpersonal adaptability was also significantly associated with performance, but the direction of the correlation was negative.

[4]   The Big Five refers to five personality factors considered by many psychologists to comprise core dimensions of personality. The five dimensions are openness to experience, conscientiousness, extraversion, agreeableness, and emotional stability.

Implications for Study Design

Our study did not include quantitative measures of adaptive job performance; therefore, our evaluation of AWALP at the individual level focused on changes in attitudes (self-efficacy, interest, and experience) about dimensions of adaptability as important training outcomes in and of themselves and as potential proximal indicators of adaptive performance. The majority of measures in this evaluation focus on six of the original eight dimensions of adaptive performance (discussed in Chapter One) emphasized most in the course: thinking creatively; dealing with changing or ambiguous situations; learning tasks, technologies, and procedures; interpersonal adaptability; cultural adaptability; and decisionmaking under stress. We assessed physical adaptability to a lesser extent and assessed handling crisis situations to a very limited extent.

Because of their potential relevance to adaptive performance, we also included several measures of individual characteristics. We measured four of the Big Five personality traits, including extraversion, conscientiousness, openness to experience, and agreeableness, using the NEO Five-Factor Inventory–3 personality inventory (Costa and McCrae, 2010); mastery and performance goal orientations (Button, Mathieu, and Zajac, 1996); general cognitive ability using the Wonderlic Contemporary Cognitive Ability Test (Wonderlic, 2012); motivation for training (i.e., perceived benefits of participating in AWALP); and a variety of demographic characteristics.

Team Adaptability
Background

Little work in organizations today is accomplished solely at the individual level; very often, individuals are expected to come together in teams to accomplish a task. While there is an abundance of studies of team effectiveness, there is much less (albeit increasing) research on the nature and determinants of team adaptability, and various conceptualizations of team adaptability have been proposed. For example, Pulakos, Dorsey, and White, 2006, defined team adaptability using six of the eight dimensions of individual adaptability (excluding physical adaptability and cultural adaptability) and postulated individual and team factors that contribute to team adaptability. Burke, Stagl, et al., 2006, defined team adaptation as "a change in team performance, in response to a salient cue or cue stream, that leads to a functional outcome for the entire team" (p. 1190). Chen, Thomas, and Wallace, 2005, suggested that individual and team adaptation involve the transfer of newly acquired skills and knowledge from one context (training) to another more complex one (a more-complex training simulation). Kozlowski et al., 1999, suggested that adaptation is a natural byproduct of successful team functioning in complex environments, in that over time and successive cycles of performance, individuals come to know and understand their places on a team, and the team as a whole develops an understanding of which team members (and accompanying knowledge, skills, abilities, and other characteristics) and processes (such as coordination) will enable the team to react to the environment productively. The team develops a repertoire of flexible responses that it can apply to relevant situations. These models explore in varying depth the process mechanisms that facilitate or impede adaptation and the individual differences that may affect those processes.

While the body of empirical findings regarding team adaptability is relatively small, it is well established that team processes, such as communication and coordination, contribute to team performance and effectiveness (e.g., Salas et al., 2008), including performance on tasks that are novel, complex, stressful, or otherwise require change (i.e., require adaptive performance) (e.g., Entin and Serfaty, 1999; Orasanu, 1990; Smith-Jentsch, Johnston, and Payne, 1998). Moreover, team training affects team processes (Salas et al., 2008). For example, Entin and Serfaty, 1999, showed that teams can be trained to engage in communication and coordination behavior that contribute to shared mental models and adaptive performance.

The importance of teams was well understood in the design of AWALP. Most of the practical exercises are conducted in teams (with teams being recomposed for each exercise). The curriculum addresses such concepts as the distinction between taskwork and teamwork (e.g., Morgan et al., 1986), and emphasizes processes, such as communication, collaboration, and coordination, to foster shared mental models and situational awareness. In addition to discussing how individuals are adaptable in the context of team activities, a central focus of AARs is how adaptability manifests at the team level.

Implications for Study Design

Our analysis included measures of the dimensions of adaptability at the team level. We asked students and guides to assess both the requirements for the dimensions of adaptive performance in team practical exercises and team effectiveness in meeting the requirements. In addition, some of our measures assessed individual student knowledge of processes associated with team effectiveness.

Leader Adaptability

Background

At the intersection of the individual and the team is the leader. This, too, has been the focus of some ongoing work. However, Kozlowski et al., 2009, noted that, while team leaders are the key to developing team capabilities, this aspect of their role is largely ignored in current leadership theory.

Noting that individual adaptability is not sufficient with regard to Army officers in particular, White et al., 2005, suggested adding a ninth dimension to the initial eight Pulakos and colleagues had identified: leading an adaptable team. Tucker and Gunther, 2009, collected critical incidents from officers and NCOs who had recently deployed (whereas those in Pulakos et al.'s original sample were collected before these conflicts began). Tucker and Gunther found that officers, in particular, described incidents relating to dealing with ambiguous or uncertain environments, although relatively few critical incidents related to the new dimension of leading an adaptable team. However, when asked for suggestions about how best to enhance the capacity for adaptability, the number of incidents pertaining to leading adaptable teams greatly increased. Other work (Zaccaro et al., 2009) suggests that team-level feedback on both process and outcome performance issues enables better performance (i.e., adaptive behavior), and this work notes that feedback emphasizing the quality of the team interaction during a mission is likely to make for a more-effective AAR. Key principles in AWALP include the ideas that leader training should focus on enhancing team development and that effective team performance can enhance leader decisionmaking.

Implications for Study Design

We developed questions to assess the intersection of the leader and the team, focusing on AWALP participants' self-efficacy for, interest in, and perceived need for behaviors that will enable them to develop and lead adaptable teams. We refer to this construct as "leader practice."

Other Methodological Considerations

Challenges to Measuring Adaptability

Adaptive performance is difficult to measure for several reasons. First, the dimensions (e.g., handling stress, thinking creatively) are largely intangible or abstract, and intangible concepts are typically measured using self-report methods, which can be subject to biases and threats to validity.

Some of these potential biases and threats to validity are illustrated in the results obtained from the method used to assess AWALP in the past. In brief, at the start of training, students were asked to respond to ten questions about their level of adaptability readiness. For example, students were asked if they were prepared or unprepared with respect to "Understanding of what it means to be adaptable." At the conclusion of training, students were provided with their pretraining responses and asked to report how they would have answered, knowing what they know now. They were then asked to report their current level of preparation having completed AWALP. Figure 2.1 provides an example of these responses.

As shown in Figure 2.1, nearly all the students felt that they understood what adaptability meant prior to training. After training, the majority realized that they were not prepared initially, and all students felt prepared moving forward. The pattern of results was similar across the ten items and suggests that students believe AWALP was highly effective in training soldiers to be adaptable.

Figure 2.1
Example of Results from Prior AWALP Evaluation

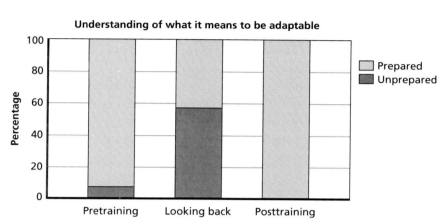

RAND *RR504-2.1*

However, there are a variety of alternative interpretations for these results:

- Questions are likely subject to *social desirability bias* in that, prior to training, respondents may not want to admit that they do not know what it means to be adaptable or may want to give the impression that they are adaptable.
- The general nature of questions, such as knowing what it means to be adaptable, may not be very instructive because respondents may not know what they do not know. In addition, similar patterns of results across items suggest that the responses do not discriminate among different constructs addressed in the course.
- The high ratings before AWALP began result in *ceiling effects*, making it difficult to demonstrate improvement or to document associations of responses with other variables, such as individual differences or other outcome measures.
- Providing students with their pretraining responses and asking them to reflect back after training presents *demand characteristics* (i.e., when respondents become aware of what the questions are investigating and change their behavior). Thus, respondents

essentially know what the "expected" answers are and may have responded accordingly.

A second reason adaptability is difficult to measure is that a comprehensive assessment can pose a significant response burden, particularly because adaptability can occur at different levels (i.e., individual, team, and the leader-team intersection). Assessing change due to the training requires administering pretraining measures, further increasing the response burden. Furthermore, because adaptability is likely correlated with a variety of individual characteristics, it is important to measure the characteristics to assess whether the impact of an intervention, such as AWALP, occurs *in addition* to the effects of the characteristics—that is, whether the intervention itself has an identifiable effect beyond characteristics that would predict adaptable behavior. However, this again adds to the measurement burden.

Finally, although there are many established and available measures of individual characteristics that are likely to be associated with adaptive performance, few measures of adaptive performance are available in the public domain. Developing reliable and valid measures requires a large number of respondents.

Addressing Challenges to Measuring Adaptability

We used a fourfold strategy to address these challenges. First, we used a combination of multiple measures of adaptive performance, including piloting new ones. The goals of doing so were to assess a range of adaptability training outcomes and to offset the weaknesses of any one method or measure, which might be subject to a particular bias, with other approaches.

Second, rather than asking general questions about students' self-perceptions of adaptability knowledge or skills, we asked about specific behaviors that are indicative of the adaptive performance dimensions. This approach was used to provide precise terms that are consistent with the Pulakos et al., 2000, taxonomy and to attempt to reduce demand characteristics and social desirability biases. We also used an objective measure of knowledge in the form of a multiple-choice test on adaptability and team concepts.

Third, for most outcome measures, we used a pretest–posttest design, rather than a posttest-only design, and included measures of individual differences that we anticipate are associated with adaptive performance. This approach enabled us to draw inferences about the impact of the intervention (AWALP training).

Fourth, to balance our relatively comprehensive approach with response burden, we focused our evaluation on the factors we consider *most critical* to adaptive performance and to the AWALP course. For example, we assessed adaptability primarily for individuals and to a lesser extent for teams, given that the goal of the course is to train adaptability at the individual and leader level rather than to train intact teams through multiple experiences. Furthermore, we included some, but not all, of the dimensions of adaptive performance in our instruments, in large part reflecting the emphasis of each dimension in the course as described in Chapter One.

Study Design

Participants

The evaluation of AWALP focused on students enrolled in three AWALP classes conducted in January, April, and August 2013 (Class 10, 11, and 12, respectively). There were 104 students across the three classes. With the exception of interviews, described in Chapter Five, participation rates in the evaluation study were close to 100 percent; three students did not complete the surveys or tests because they arrived late to the course or left early. Some students did not answer all the questions; therefore, we have missing values for some analyses.

On average, student participants were 31.5 years old ($SD = 6.28$) and had 10.83 years of service ($SD = 5.68$). Table 2.1 shows other demographic characteristics of the students.

Nine of the students in one of the AWALP classes were operational advisors, who were included in the class as part of their training to work with Army and joint force units to predict and respond to asymmetric threats and methods. Operational advisors' responses to the measures used in the evaluation did not differ from other students,

Table 2.1
Student Demographic Characteristics

Category	Demographic	Percent
Rank	Specialist or sergeant (E4–5)	15
	Staff sergeant (E6)	31
	Sergeant first class (E7)	25
	Master sergeant, first sergeant, sergeant major, or command sergeant major (E8–9)	18
	Officer (2LT–LTC)	12
Career field	Infantry	42
	Armor	13
	Field Artillery	12
	Military Intelligence	9
	Military Police Corps	7
	Other	17
Highest degree	High school or GED	18
	Some college	46
	Two-year college degree	10
	Bachelor's or graduate degree	26

NOTE: Percentages may not sum to 100 due to rounding.

so they were included in the analyses. However, they were not included in the assessment of graduates' application of AWALP principles on the job reported in Chapter Five.

In addition to student participants, seven guides participated in one component of the research in which they evaluated team performance effectiveness, described in more detail below and in Chapter Four. Supervisors participated in follow-up interviews, which are described in Chapter Five.

Table 2.2
Measures, Methods, Constructs, and Schedule of Administration

Measure	Methods	Timing	Constructs	Class Administered		
				10	11	12
Reactions	Survey	Posttraining	Satisfaction with training	•	•	•
Affective training outcomes (attitudes)	Survey	Pre- and posttraining	Self-efficacy for behaviors associated with adaptive performance and leading adaptable teams, interest in engaging in these behaviors, and frequency of engaging in these behaviors	•	•	•
Learning (cognitive)	Paper-and-pencil test	Pre- and posttraining	Declarative knowledge of adaptability and team concepts	•	•	•
Learning (behavioral)	Survey of peer ratings of individuals	After phase 1 and phase 2	Requirements for and effectiveness of adaptive performance	•		
	Survey—students' ratings of teams	After exercises on days 3, 5, and 7			•	•
	Survey—guides' ratings of teams				•	•
Application of AWALP concepts on the job	Interviews	Three and six months posttraining	Graduate and supervisor reports	•	•	•
Individual characteristics	Paper-and-pencil test; survey	Pretraining	General cognitive ability
Personality traits
Learning goal orientation
Motivation for training (perceived benefits of AWALP)
Demographic characteristics	•	•	

Methods, Measures, and Procedures

Table 2.2 shows the measures, methods, and constructs measured in the evaluation, along with the schedule of administration of the measures. Pretraining measures were collected the evening before AWALP began ("day 0"), and posttraining measures were collected on the last day of AWALP ("day 10"). Data collection took approximately 80 minutes on day 0 and 45 minutes on day 10. As shown in Table 2.2, other outcomes (peer ratings and ratings of teams) were collected at various points throughout the course, and application of course principles on the job was measured three or six months following AWALP. Measures were administered using paper-and-pencil instruments. For most measures, there were no differences by class, so analyses were conducted across all three classes.

Some of the individual characteristics measures (general cognitive ability, personality traits) are from commercial instruments. We used these measures in all three classes. In contrast, we took an experimental approach with measures we developed for this evaluation. For example, we modified methods (e.g., for attitudes) or discontinued measures (e.g., peer ratings) after learning from the experience of the first class. Furthermore, we did not use a measure (e.g., team ratings) in every class to balance the comprehensiveness of the evaluation with response burden.

The commercial instruments used in the evaluation are publicly available. However, to maintain the integrity of future evaluations of AWALP, neither the knowledge test nor the measures of attitudes toward adaptability that we developed for this evaluation are published. These measures may be obtained by contacting AWG.

In Chapters Three through Five, we describe the methods and measures in more detail and present the results of the evaluation for the measures shown in column 1 of Table 2.2.

CHAPTER THREE

Reactions Toward AWALP and Attitudes Toward Adaptability

This chapter reports on reactions to the course, measured at the end of training, and changes in attitudes toward adaptive performance, measured at the beginning and end of the course.

Reactions to AWALP

Method

Reactions were measured in the posttraining survey. The survey included 28 close-ended questions assessing students' views of course content, delivery, and structure and six open-ended questions asking students to elaborate on some of their responses. Examples of close-ended questions include "AWALP guides effectively facilitated course exercises," and "Attending AWALP was a good use of my time." Some of the questions were based on White et al., 2005, and Straus, Shanley, Yeung, et al., 2011. Most of the close-ended questions used six-point response scales, with options ranging from 1 = strongly disagree to 6 = strongly agree. A small number of questions provided response scales with three options (e.g., too much, about right, too little; see Figure 3.2). The questions are shown in Appendix B.

Results

Students reported high levels of satisfaction with AWALP. Figure 3.1 shows the average scores on responses to items (a number of which were a composite of multiple survey questions) about course

Figure 3.1
Average Ratings: Course Delivery and Overall Satisfaction

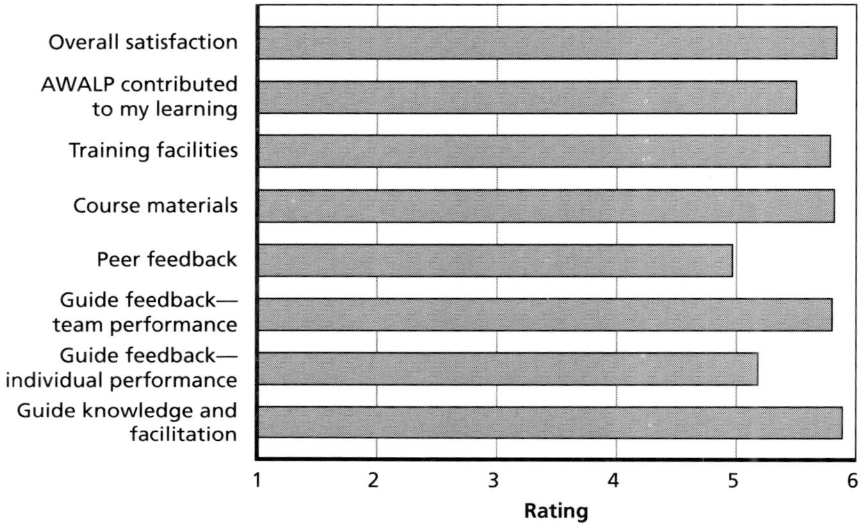

NOTES: Some aspects of satisfaction were measured with multiple-item scales,
including guide knowledge and facilitation (three items), AWALP contributed to
learning (11 items), and overall satisfaction (four items). Coefficient α values for these
scales were 0.79, 0.93, and 0.88, respectively. Coefficient α is a measure of the internal
consistency reliability of a set of items. It typically ranges from zero to one, with
higher values indicating greater reliability. Coefficient α values of 0.80 and higher are
generally considered satisfactory, although values are influenced by the number of
items on a scale; thus, a scale with a few items will typically have a lower α than a
scale with many items.
RAND RR504-3.1

delivery and overall satisfaction in the course. Average scores ranged
from approximately 5 to 6. The highest rating was given to the guides
(guide knowledge and facilitation), closely followed by several other
aspects of course delivery and overall satisfaction. Feedback from
guides about team performance was also given high ratings, but ratings for guide feedback about individual performance were lower, suggesting that the course focuses more on the former.

"AWALP contributed to my learning" (the second bar from the
top in Figure 3.1) is a combination of answers to items dealing with
learning different dimensions of adaptive performance and various
leader practices. The average rating was 5.50, and each component

question also had a high rating, ranging from about 5.27 to 5.60. To gain additional insight about how the course contributed to learning, a follow-up, open-ended question asked students to identify the two topics for which they changed the most and the two topics for which they changed the least as a result of the course; it further asked them to explain the reasons for their choices. Frequencies of "top two" and "bottom two" responses are shown in Figure 3.2.

While the areas of most and least improvement were distributed across all response options, AARs stand out. Fifty percent of the students identified AARs as one of the two areas in which they learned the most. The most frequent explanations for "why" included (in order of frequency) that the AWALP method promotes better communication, provides a better way to plan, facilitates the use of open-ended questions, allows teams to go deeper, and promotes a focus on learning. Creative thinking, identified by 25 percent of students, was also a frequently mentioned "top two" area. The most frequently mentioned comments for creative thinking were that AWALP taught graduates to keep an open mind and how to correctly analyze problems. Among

Figure 3.2
Areas of Most and Least Improvement

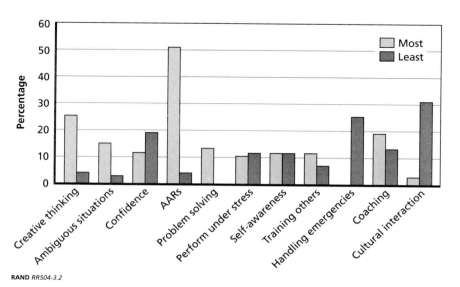

"bottom two" topics, cultural interaction was the area most frequently mentioned (by over 30 percent of students). By far, the most frequently mentioned reason for this choice (not only in the cultural area but in all areas of least learning) was that students felt that they already had the skills or attribute prior to attending AWALP (e.g., "Interacting with different cultures was already a strong point").

All students reported that they would recommend AWALP to others; the most common reasons were the course content and training approach. After students reported whether they would recommend AWALP to others, which was one of the questions on the "Overall satisfaction" scale, they were then asked to respond to an open-ended question about why or why not (note that all students gave an "agree" response to this question). We used content analysis to group responses into categories. Results are shown in Figure 3.3. Among those who answered the question, the most common reason for recommending the course was because of the adaptability concepts they learned (e.g., "learned effective AAR," and "fostered creative thinking"). Other common responses were that students valued the training approach (e.g., "introduces an entirely new and more benefi-

Figure 3.3
Reasons Students Would Recommend AWALP to Others

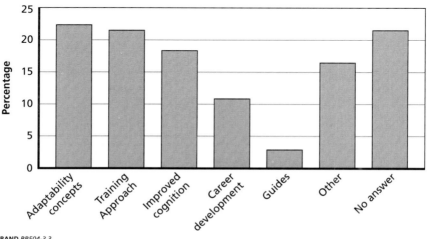

cial teaching/learning style") or thought that AWALP improved their cognition (e.g., "learned better techniques to think" and "makes you open your mind"). Eleven percent of the students responded that what they learned in the course will help them develop in their careers (e.g., "it helps develop leadership traits rarely, if ever, trained outside [of AWALP]"). Finally, 3 percent of the students said they would recommend the course based on the quality of the guides.[1]

Students were highly satisfied with the course structure. Figure 3.4 shows frequencies of responses to questions about the course structure. Results show that the preponderance of students thought the course was "about right" with respect to course length, classroom time, difficulty level of course content, and difficulty of course exercises. The area with the greatest perceived need for change was in course length, for which 13 percent of students thought that the course should be

Figure 3.4
Ratings of Course Structure

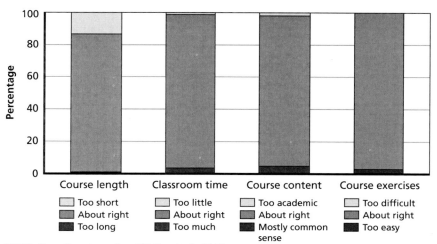

NOTE: Questions based on White et al., 2005.

RAND RR504-3.4

---

[1] The "other" category primarily comprised comments that, rather than providing specific reasons for recommending the course, demonstrate respondents' enthusiasm for the course by recommending widespread Army attendance or reaffirming that students thought "it was a great course."

longer. As the results below suggest, requests for a longer course can be interpreted as a positive sentiment about the course; this interpretation is also consistent with patterns of overall satisfaction ratings, which were very favorable among all students (see Figure 3.1), but were significantly higher for students who thought that the course should be longer than for students who though the course was "about right."[2]

Recommendations for improvements to AWALP were directed largely at making the course even better, as opposed to identifying and resolving weaknesses. Figure 3.5 shows results of analyzing responses to an open-ended question asking students for suggested changes to the course, which were coded into categories representing common themes. Twenty-eight percent of students reported no need for change, and 24 percent did not answer the question. In the "change training" (17 percent) and "add training" (12 percent) columns, the majority of responses were general (e.g., "maybe more shooting" for change training and "make the course longer" for add training), but the overall theme of these comments was to enhance an already effective course. Nine percent of the students recommended that students remove rank and patches during the course to put all participants on

Figure 3.5
Suggestions to Improve AWALP

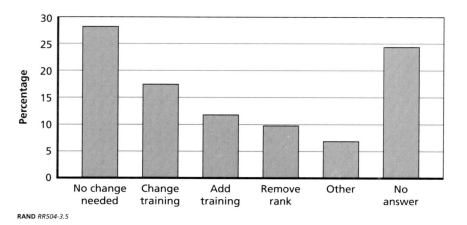

RAND RR504-3.5

---

[2] $t(85) = 3.36, p < 0.01.$

a level playing field; as one student put it, "to let everyone know that rank has nothing to do with one's creative thinking." The "other" category contains responses that were not specifically about course content or delivery; for example, one student suggested being more selective about who attends.

Other common requests for improvements can be found in the "change training" category. In particular, five students suggested making the capstone exercise more challenging (e.g., "[add] more stress"; "did not push threshold of failure"; "more time, more freedom of movement, more negative reactions"; "[make] real world, with real intelligence gathered"). Three recommended encouraging more individual involvement in training exercises (e.g., "[give] more individuals more opportunities to be put on the spot, i.e., to speak, lead, solve problems"). Only two students thought the course was too long.

Students anticipated that leader buy-in and command climate would pose challenges to applying adaptability concepts on the job. Students were asked in an open-ended question about challenges they expected in applying AWALP concepts. Responses were coded into categories based on common themes. Nearly two-thirds of the students identified one or more challenges. About 17 percent of the students said they anticipated no challenges, and an equal number skipped the question.

Leader buy-in was the most frequently mentioned challenge, a response identified by nearly one-third of the students (see Figure 3.6). Some expressed this sentiment quite succinctly (e.g., my challenge is "my higher chain of command)." Others provided more details. For example, one student said "I will want to push new ideas too quickly into my training plans. My biggest challenge will be to pace that and sell my leadership on what I am trying to accomplish."

Twenty percent of students responded, somewhat more generally, that they anticipated "command climate" to be a challenge. For example, one student talked about the need for "fostering command climate." Another said "there is the challenge of changing the Army culture to open up to this way of training." Collapsing "leadership buy-in" and "command climate" responses, over one-half of the graduates

Figure 3.6
Anticipated Challenges to Implementing AWALP Principles

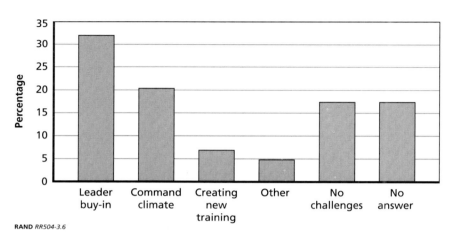

expressed the sentiment that it is a challenge to get the Army to accept the AWALP way of training.

Seven percent of students anticipated challenges designing new training. One student commented, "My first few training ideas will be the most difficult to construct. I will build from those successes/ failures in order to create better ambiguous situations and foster learning environments." We also categorized 5 percent of the responses into an "other" category. For example, one graduate commented that there would be time and resource limitations that would restrict the design of AWALP training.

Despite the challenges that students foresaw, we also detected a sense of determination and spirit in responses expressed by almost one-third of students. Although not shown in Figure 3.6, 13 students volunteered that they would personally take on anticipated challenges, working to persuade others of the value of implementing AWALP principles. Eleven students went further, expressing confidence that the challenges could be overcome, sometimes by persuading others and sometimes by their own determination, e.g., "the only real challenge is how creative I am willing to get."

Summary of Reactions to Training

Students had extremely favorable reactions to AWALP, both overall and with respect to specific aspects of the course. Furthermore, students indicated that they would recommend the course to others precisely because of its unique teaching approach. Even among the minority of students who suggested course improvements, most indicated that they wanted to make a good course even better. Despite these positive reactions, nearly two-thirds of the students saw challenges in applying the principles they learned in AWALP when they returned to their units.

It is worth noting that reactions to AWALP are much more favorable than reactions to Army institutional leader training reported elsewhere. For example, the Center for Army Leadership Annual Survey of Army Leadership (CASAL) (Riley et al., 2013) reported that in response to a global question about institutional training in 2012, 58 percent of active-duty leaders rated the training as very effective or effective in preparing them for leadership, and 20 percent rated it as ineffective. In response to questions about specific Army courses and schools from 2008 to 2012, 46 percent of respondents reported that courses improved their leadership capabilities; 53 percent found the content relevant to leadership responsibilities in their next job; and 65 percent found the content was up to date. Although these questions are not identical to those asked in the AWALP evaluation, it is clear that the degree of satisfaction with AWALP is substantially higher.

Attitudes Toward Adaptive Performance

Method

We assessed affective training outcomes by measuring attitudes toward adaptive performance and changes in the attitudes using self-report measures administered pre- and posttraining. We used or adapted published items from Ployhart and Bliese, 2006; Pulakos et al., 2000; Pulakos et al., 2002; and White et al., 2005, and supplemented them with original items. Items measured six of the eight dimensions of adaptive performance (creative thinking; dealing with ambiguous situations; learning tasks, technologies, and procedures; interpersonal adaptability; cultural adaptability; and decisionmaking under stress). The survey included two or three items about each of these dimensions. Examples include "Come up with alternative courses of action that others may not have considered" (for creative thinking) and "Deal with a situation where things are not 'black and white'" (for dealing with ambiguous situations). In addition, based on topics addressed in the AWALP curriculum, we developed seven items about putting adaptability concepts into leader practice, such as "Coach subordinates," "Delegate responsibility to others on tasks on which they might fail," and "Seek input from subordinates about a complex decision."

Note that the items do not ask directly about adaptability in AWALP or a specific adaptive performance dimension; rather, they ask about a variety of more-general situations that relate to those dimensions. The goals of this approach are to reduce social desirability biases and potential ceiling effects, demand characteristics (responding with what respondents see as the "expected" answer), and other issues related to students not necessarily knowing what adaptability means.

Following Pulakos et al., 2002, we measured three aspects or attributes of attitudes: (1) frequency with which students engage in each behavior or situation in their jobs (pretraining) or feel that they should engage in the behavior or situation in their jobs (posttraining), (2) interest in engaging in the behavior or situation, and (3) self-efficacy for the behavior or situation.[3] Unlike Pulakos et al., 2002, which examined whether experience, interest, and self-efficacy predicted performance ratings by supervisors, we administered the questions before and after training to assess changes in attitudes following AWALP. Accordingly, we revised the posttraining question about experience or frequency to reflect the need for adaptability behaviors.

Response options for questions about frequency included "never," "a few times/year," "monthly," "weekly," and "daily." Response options for questions about interest and self-efficacy used six-point scales rang-

---

[3] In the first class of students, we also asked about the importance of engaging in each behavior or activity. Results showed that most students thought adaptability was important to their jobs coming into the course; thus, there were ceiling effects for responses prior to training, leaving little room for improvement. Consequently, we eliminated this attribute for subsequent classes to reduce response burden.

ing from 1 = strongly disagree to 6 = strongly agree. Table 3.1 shows the format for the questions.[4]

For measures of frequency, we compared the distribution of the differences between responses pre- and posttraining using an example item of each adaptive performance dimension.[5] For interest and self-efficacy, we present the mean ratings of the items measuring each dimension and leader practice. Statistical tests were directional, reflecting the expectation that attitudes would become more positive from pre- to posttraining. We also adjusted the alpha level for multiple tests using a Bonferroni correction.

Results

There was improvement in almost all aspects of attitudes toward adaptive performance. As Table 3.2 shows, after the course, students

Table 3.1
Format for Questions About Attitudes Toward Adaptive Performance Pre- and Posttraining

Attribute	Instructions
Frequency	How often is this activity a part of your job? (pretraining) How often do you think you should be doing this activity on your job? (posttraining)
Interest	I would like doing this task or working in situations that require this activity (pre- and posttraining)
Self-efficacy	I am capable of carrying out each activity, today, without any additional training (pre- and posttraining)

[4] Coefficient α for the self-efficacy and interest scales was generally high, ranging from 0.65 to 0.87, indicating that the scales were internally consistent. The Likert-type response scales used for these questions can approximate a continuous variable; however, coefficient α is not applicable for the frequency scales, which used such response options as "never" and "monthly," and reactions to course structure in the current evaluation, which used such response options as "too much," "too little," and "about right").

[5] Only one item was used because responses to frequencies cannot be added together to create a single measure. However, we analyzed all the items to verify that results were similar for the different items measuring each construct. This was the case for the dimensions of adaptability, but there were differences in the distributions of answers for the items measuring leader practice. Therefore, we report the leader practice items separately.

Table 3.2
Summary of Changes in Attitudes

Dimension	Self-efficacy	Interest in performing	Need in current job
Creative thinking	X	X	X
Ambiguous situations	X	X	X
Learning	X	X	X
Interpersonal	X	X	X
Cultural	X	X	X
Decisionmaking under stress	X	X	X
Leader practice	X	X	Varied

thought they were better at being adaptable in all dimensions and in leader practice. They also reported greater interest in adaptability than they had before the course. In addition, at the end of the course, students saw their jobs as requiring more adaptive performance with respect to all the dimensions of adaptability and most leader practice behaviors. Thus, after the course, students not only sensed a change in their own capabilities and interests regarding adaptive performance, but they saw their work contexts in a different light.

The following sections present our results for each of the three attributes of students' attitudes.

Self-Efficacy for Adaptive Performance

Students' responses indicate substantial increases in self-efficacy for adaptive performance from the beginning to the end of the course. We used paired t-tests to compare pretraining and posttraining ratings. Figure 3.7 shows average scores. On average, students reported "agree somewhat" before training and "agree" responses after training. The increase in self-efficacy was statistically significant at $p < 0.001$ for all dimensions and for leader practice. These results are consistent with Roselle, 2013, which compared pretraining and posttraining self-report for adaptability behaviors and preferences among AWALP students with a control group that did not participate in the course.

Figure 3.7
Self-Efficacy Ratings Pre- and Posttraining

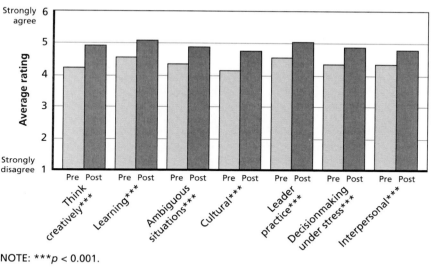

NOTE: ***$p < 0.001$.

RAND RR504-3.7

The results in Figure 3.7 are presented in decreasing order of effect size, which indicates the practical significance of the findings.[6] Effect sizes for the differences between pre- and posttraining ratings were large for thinking creatively; ambiguous situations; and learning tasks, technologies, and procedures and were moderate for the remaining constructs.

As discussed in the method section above, the questions about self-efficacy assess improvement from the course indirectly by asking students to rate their skills before and after the course and then ana-

---

[6] Effect sizes, not shown in Figure 3.7, estimate the strength of the relationship between variables, in contrast to significance levels, which reflect the probability that the observed relationship could have occurred by chance. When sample sizes are large, a statistical test can be significant, even if the size of the test statistic (e.g., a correlation of 0.10) is too small to be considered practically important. For t-tests, Cohen, 1988, describes effect sizes of 0.8 as large, 0.5 as moderate, and 0.2 as small. For changes in self-efficacy, effect sizes (d) were 0.78 for creative thinking; 0.69 for learning tasks, technologies, and procedures; 0.64 for dealing with ambiguous situations; and 0.61 for cultural adaptability, and d ranged from 0.50 to 0.54 for the remaining constructs.

lyzing the difference, while controlling for student characteristics. The reaction survey also included items representing a different approach, one that directly asked students to rate how much the AWALP contributed to learning dimensions of adaptive performance and related constructs. Figure 3.8 shows the distribution of responses ("strongly agree," "agree," etc.), as well as the average rating of each item. The right vertical axis ("Average rating") tracks the mean scores line.

Results for both self-efficacy and these direct responses are generally consistent. For example, for self-efficacy, thinking creatively and dealing with ambiguity have larger changes than do cultural adaptability and decisionmaking under stress; similarly, the direct measures of creative thinking and ambiguous situations have higher means than do cultural adaptability and decisionmaking under stress. However, it is also important to note that the average ratings for the direct measures in Figure 3.8 are substantially higher than the average posttraining ratings of self-efficacy in Figure 3.7. This suggests that our approach to

Figure 3.8
Direct Questions About AWALP Impact

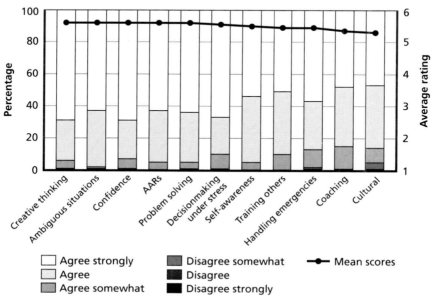

measuring improvement indirectly was successful at avoiding ceiling effects, even in this very popular course.

Interest in Adaptive Performance

Students' responses also show significantly greater interest in being adaptable following AWALP (see Figure 3.9). As with the findings for self-efficacy, students reported, on average, "agree somewhat" before training and "agree" responses after training. Results of paired t-tests showed statistically significant increases for all dimensions and for leader practice. Results show a large effect size for ambiguous situations and moderate to small effect sizes for the remaining constructs.[7]

Figure 3.9
Interest Ratings Pre- and Posttraining

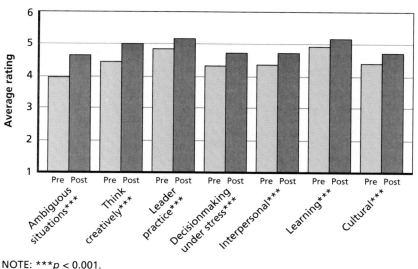

NOTE: ***$p < 0.001$.
RAND RR504-3.9

---

[7] The effect size was 0.77 for ambiguous situations, 0.44 for decisionmaking under stress, and 0.47 for leader practice. The size ranged from 0.27 to 0.37 for the remaining constructs.

Explanatory Variables

Results show substantial improvement in self-efficacy and interest, even after accounting for students' individual differences that are associated with adaptive performance. We used analysis of variance to examine the association of individual characteristics with changes in self-efficacy and interest. These analyses indicate whether individual differences are associated with training outcomes and whether the changes in outcomes appear to be the result of the course or of student characteristics (or of both). We analyzed Big Five personality traits, including openness to experience, conscientiousness, and extraversion, as well as other dispositional and demographic characteristics, including learning goal orientation (mastery and performance orientations), motivation for training, and time in service. We eliminated some variables, including age, which was highly correlated with time in service; achievement orientation, which was highly correlated with conscientiousness; and agreeableness, which was not internally consistent.[8]

Results show that the increase in both self-efficacy and interest remain statistically significant and large for all dimensions of adaptive performance and leader practice when controlling for students' individual characteristics. There were main effects for some of the individual characteristics, particularly mastery learning goal orientation, extraversion, and time in service for both self-efficacy and interest outcomes. In most cases, we found evidence that students with high scores on these traits or with longer tenure in the Army reported higher self-efficacy and interest for several of the outcomes when measured at pretraining but not at posttraining. There were also a small number of interactions between time (i.e., from pretest to posttest) and between some of the individual differences characteristics, indicating that the increase in self-efficacy and interest for some dimensions of adaptive performance depended on student characteristics, but the interactions were few and not systematic (see Appendix C).

In addition to examining the association of individual characteristics with changes in attitudes, we conducted hierarchical regression

---

[8]   Coefficient α for agreeableness = 0.68. Coefficient α for the other Big Five scales ranged from 0.77 to 0.82.

analyses to assess whether individual characteristics could account for self-efficacy and interest in the outcomes measured at the end of training, over and above the pretraining measures of self-efficacy and interest. The increase in variance explained for self-efficacy measures was statistically significant for only three of the outcomes: creative thinking; learning tasks, technologies, and procedures; and decisionmaking under stress. For these outcomes, the increase in variance explained was largely due to conscientiousness and, in the case of decisionmaking under stress, by time in service, although time in service was negatively associated with self-efficacy for decisionmaking under stress at the end of training.

Overall, the results indicate that training outcomes improved substantially, regardless of individual differences. This suggests that measurement of individual differences is not needed to demonstrate the benefits of AWALP for changes in learners' attitudes toward adaptive performance, and we would not recommend selecting participants for AWALP based on individual differences or revising the course to account for these characteristics. However, because we measured learner attitudes rather than performance, these results may depart from findings of other studies that show consistent associations of characteristics, such as cognitive ability, conscientiousness, and extraversion with performance. Therefore, even though individual characteristics did not contribute to the variance explained for most of the posttraining outcomes, it is worthwhile to continue to measure individual differences if the goal is to assess transfer of training, i.e., the impact of AWALP (or adaptability training more broadly) on subsequent job performance when prior research shows that individual differences do matter. We address this in more detail when discussing suggestions for future research in Chapter Six.

Need for Adaptive Performance

In addition to changes in students' perceptions about their capabilities and interests, students' views of their job requirements changed following AWALP. The next five figures show results for the perceived need for adaptive performance. In each figure, the stacked bar on the left of each pair shows the percentages of responses in each category (daily, monthly, etc.) before training, indicating how much students report *currently engaging* in the behavior. The stacked bar on the right of each pair shows comparable responses after training, indicating how often students think they *should be engaging* in the behavior. Wilcoxon Signed Rank tests were used to compare the differences in responses. Appendix D shows the degree of individual change in responses (percentage of students whose pre-post responses did not change, changed by one response category, by two response categories, etc.). Note that, while we had multiple items for each dimension, the figures show results for only one item. Unless noted, the items measuring each dimension of adaptability not presented below showed similar patterns of results.

Results suggest increased need for all dimensions of adaptive performance in students' current jobs. These changes can be seen by the increasing darker gray and black segments in each pair of stacked bars in the figures. Dimensions showing the greatest shift are shown in Figure 3.10; those with a smaller but still statistically significant shift are shown in Figure 3.11. For example, in Figure 3.10, responses to a

Figure 3.10
Need for Creative Thinking, Learning, and Cultural Adaptability in Current Job

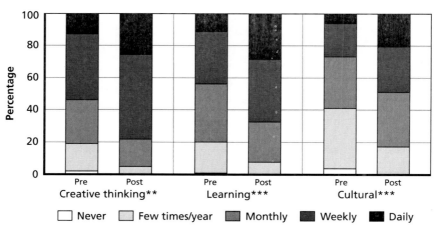

NOTE: $**p < 0.01$; $***p < 0.001$.
RAND RR504-3.10

Figure 3.11
Need for Dealing with Ambiguity, Interpersonal Adaptability, and Decisionmaking Under Stress in Current Job

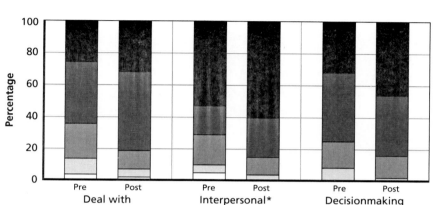

NOTE: *$p < 0.05$; **$p < 0.01$.

RAND RR504-3.11

question about creativity (i.e., "solve problems for which there are no easy or straightforward answers") before AWALP show that 41 percent of students reported engaging in this behavior on a weekly basis; after AWALP, 52 percent reported that they should engage in this behavior on a weekly basis. Likewise, 13 percent reported engaging in this aspect of creative thinking on a daily basis before AWALP, and 27 percent reported that they should engage in this behavior daily after AWALP. The degree of the differences between the beginning and the end of the course shows, for example, that 16 percent of students changed their response by two or more categories in a positive direction (e.g., from "monthly" to "daily" or "from a few times per year" to "weekly"), 32 percent changed their response by one category, 39 percent did not change their response, and so on (see Appendix D).

Note, however, that for cultural adaptability, the effects are different depending on the item. For "Take action to learn about social groups other than my own"—the item shown in Figure 3.10—the effect was much stronger than for items addressing national culture,

such as "Develop relationships with people from different countries"—
the item shown in Figure 3.12. These differences are not surprising
given that the focus on cultural adaptability in AWALP is fairly broad
and is not specifically on national culture.

**Results also suggest an increase in the perceived need for
engaging in most of the behaviors associated with leader practice.**
These include seeking consensus from subordinates on complex decisions, seeking input from subordinates on complex decisions, training others to solve complex problems, delegating tasks to others on
which they might fail, and conducting AARs (Figure 3.13). Shifts for
two of these behaviors—seeking subordinate consensus and conducting AARs—are particularly dramatic. Prior to training, 44 percent of
students reported that they sought consensus from subordinates on a
weekly or daily basis; after training, 79 percent report the need to do
so weekly or daily. Likewise, 46 percent of students reported that they
conduct AARs weekly or daily; following AWALP, 71 percent reported
that they should conduct AARs weekly or daily. This shift in responses
for AARs is consistent with the students' responses shown in Figure 3.2
about the positive impact of AWALP on AARs.

Figure 3.12
**Need for Cultural Adaptability (People from Different Countries) in Current
Job**

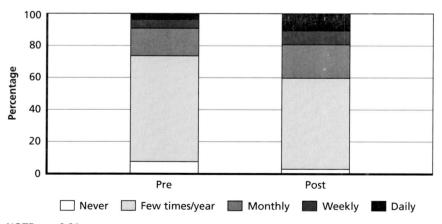

NOTE: $p < 0.01$.

Figure 3.13
Significant Shifts in Need for Leader Behaviors in Current Job

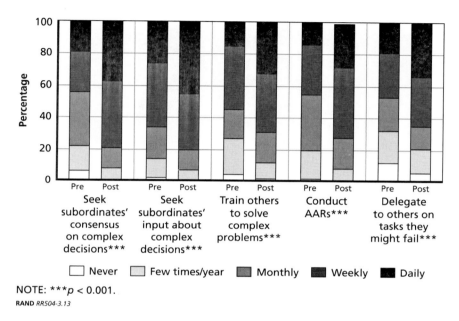

NOTE: ***$p < 0.001$.

RAND RR504-3.13

In contrast, the perceived need for two other behaviors associated with leader practice in the current job did not significantly change after AWALP. The distributions of responses showed that students already coach subordinates and train others to work in collaborative teams (Figure 3.14).

Interpreting differences between "currently engage" and "should engage" is somewhat equivocal because we did not ask the question in the same way in both surveys. If we had asked participants how often they should engage in the behavior in the pretraining survey, their ratings might have been higher, resulting in potentially smaller differences. In fact, we revised the surveys for ongoing evaluation of the course so that both the pre- and posttraining surveys ask participants how often they "should" engage in the behavior. Use of the revised surveys by AWG in a subsequent AWALP class showed perceptions of increased need for all the dimensions of adaptability and most aspects

Figure 3.14
Nonsignificant Shifts in Need for Leader Behaviors in Current Job

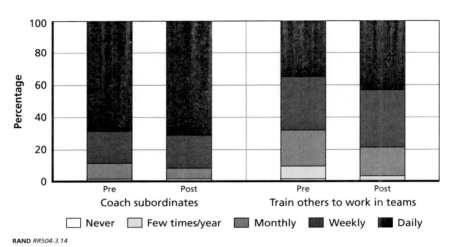

of leader practice, with the magnitude of changes from pretraining to posttraining similar to the results reported here.

Conclusions

This chapter provides strong evidence of student satisfaction with AWALP in terms of course content, structure, and delivery. All students reported that they would recommend the course to others.

Results also document changes in learners with respect to affective training outcomes (i.e., attitudes) as a result of taking the course. First, responses show substantial increases in self-efficacy for adaptability, indicating that students felt more capable in all dimensions of adaptive performance and in putting adaptability concepts into leader practice. Second, students were significantly more interested in working in situations that require adaptability. Moreover, improvements in self-efficacy and interest were substantial even after accounting for individual differences in characteristics associated with adaptive performance. Third, results suggest that students recognized a greater need for engaging in most of the adaptability and leader behaviors when returning to their current jobs.

As for future evaluation, the items used to measure attitudes addressed a series of general situations that relate to the dimensions of adaptive performance and the leadership of others. Therefore, the questions have general applicability not only in AWALP but also in other courses that train for adaptability.

CHAPTER FOUR

Results: Learning

This chapter reports on measures of cognitive and behavioral learning in AWALP based on knowledge tests of course concepts and observations of adaptability behaviors.

Knowledge of Course Concepts

Method

While gaining declarative knowledge is not a main course goal, some mastery of adaptability concepts is a prerequisite for understanding the course material and for teaching others about adaptive performance. Using course materials, and in collaboration with two of the course guides, we developed a pool of 35 multiple-choice items of knowledge about AWALP concepts. We attempted to construct a test with a range of item difficulty levels and representing the breadth of topics covered in the course. For example, items assessed knowledge of the definition of adaptability, how dimensions of adaptive performance correspond to definitions or descriptions of behaviors, and ways to develop dimensions of adaptability when designing training or leading teams. Each question had four response options.

The test was piloted with other course guides and several Army Fellows at RAND to assess whether the items were understandable and at an appropriate level of difficulty and how long it took to complete the test. We used these responses to revise or omit questions, resulting in a 30-item test (for example, a large number of incorrect responses to an item suggested that it was unclear, did not reflect material taught in the course, or was too difficult).

Two items that many students answered incorrectly were eliminated after the test was given because further examination indicated that the questions were ambiguous or did not match the content addressed in the course. Thus, scores are based on 28 items. The test was administered on day 0 and again on day 10.

Results
Results showed increased student knowledge of AWALP concepts. We used analysis of variance to analyze the change in pretraining and posttraining knowledge test scores, controlling for general cognitive ability and highest level of education. Average scores on the knowledge test were 60 percent correct pretraining (SD = 12.50) and 76 percent correct posttraining (SD = 13.90). The increase in scores was statistically significant. General cognitive ability was strongly and positively associated with scores on the pretest and posttest, but there was no interaction between the change in knowledge test scores and general cognitive ability.[1] Likewise, highest level of education was positively associated with scores on both the pretest and posttest, but there was no interaction of the change in test scores with level of education.[2] **Thus, student knowledge improved regardless of general cognitive ability or education and suggests that AWALP was successful at fostering knowledge gain for a wide range of students.**[3]

---

[1] In the analysis for cognitive ability, for the change in pretraining and posttraining knowledge test scores, $F(1,96)$ = 139.82, p < 0.001, and the effect size d = 1.29, which is a very large effect. For cognitive ability, $F(1,96)$ = 17.53, p < 0.001, and the effect sizes (r) were 0.41 for both the pretest and posttest, which is a moderate to large effect. For the interaction of test scores and cognitive ability, $F(1,96)$ < 1, not significant.

[2] In the analysis for education, for the change in pretraining and posttraining knowledge test scores, $F(1,94)$ = 96.95, p < 0.001. For education, $F(3,94)$ = 4.57, p < 0.01. For the interaction of test scores and education, $F(1,94)$ < 1, not significant.

[3] Although we do not have data to determine how representative AWALP students are of the Army at large, students' scores on the Wonderlic Contemporary Cognitive Ability Test are generally comparable to national workforce norms.

Figure 4.1 shows the distribution of differences scores (i.e., posttest score minus pretest scores). Eighty-six percent of the students showed increased declarative knowledge (i.e., had difference scores greater than zero), while 14 percent performed no better or worse on the posttest. The average difference was 16 percent (median = 14 percent). There were no obvious patterns of responses among students who performed worse (e.g., students did not select the same response for every question, which would have suggested that they did not take the test seriously).[4]

Peer Evaluations

Method

In the first of the three classes we evaluated, we experimented with peer evaluations as a behavioral measure of individual adaptive performance. We designed an approach based on the peer evaluation proce-

Figure 4.1
Distribution of Change Scores on Knowledge Test

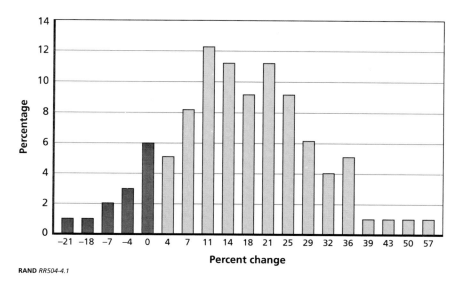

RAND RR504-4.1

---

[4] Removing these scores increases the average score only to 78 percent.

dures used at the U.S. Military Academy. Our procedure asked students to anonymously rate three of their peers on five adaptive performance dimensions at the halfway point (phase 1) and at the end of the course (phase 2). In an effort to eliminate uninformed or potentially biased evaluations, we gave each rater six names and asked them to select three of the students with whom they had worked during AWALP exercises and whom they did not know before coming to AWALP.

The constructs covered in the peer review included how much students showed flexibility in dealing with other team members, had innovative ideas, interacted effectively with others who have different values and customs, responded easily to changes in the situation, and remained calm under pressure. There was one item for each construct, and the items provided examples of relevant behaviors, e.g., for creative thinking, examples included "Had innovative ideas (including 'connected the dots' and presented unique approaches or courses of action)." As elsewhere in the evaluation, six-point scales were used, with choices from "strongly agree" to "strongly disagree." In addition, raters had an option to indicate "not applicable" for exercises they felt did not call for the behavior.

Results
Students gave high ratings of adaptive performance to their peers, which did not change significantly over time. On average, students gave their peers ratings of approximately 5 across dimensions (Figure 4.2). These ratings were somewhat higher than students' self-efficacy ratings at the end of training reported earlier. The results also indicate that, in contrast to self-ratings, adaptive performance did not increase between the midpoint of the course (phase 1) and at the end of the course (phase 2). In fact, while generally not statistically significant, average peer ratings decreased somewhat in all five areas.

While the results suggest that adaptive performance did not increase between the two phases, there are alternative plausible explanations for the peer review results, making interpretation of the findings problematic. One difficulty is that students cannot be good evaluators of other students until they have some interactions with them (which is why we waited until day 5 for the first measurement). Thus, significant

Figure 4.2
Class 10 Peer Evaluations after Phase 1 and Phase 2

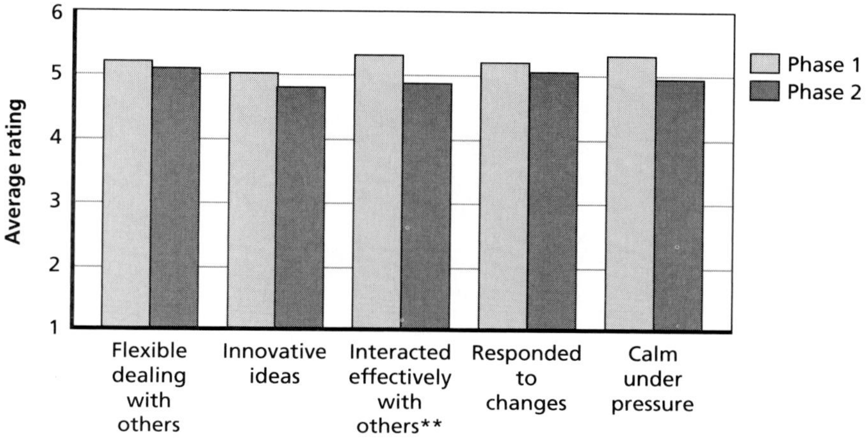

NOTE: **$p < 0.01$.

RAND RR504-4.2

improvement in adaptive performance might occur in the early part of the course but would go undetected by peer evaluations. Alternatively, ratings may reflect social desirability bias, and ceiling effects limit the possibility of higher scores over time. Another issue is that the nature of the activities differs significantly in the first and second halves of the course, making an evaluation of performance during each period difficult to compare. During the first phase, classroom activities are mixed, with relatively straightforward and focused field exercises; in the second phase, students are asked to engage in much more complex field problems. A third issue is that student raters are themselves learning during the course, becoming more educated and discriminating and, as a result, may be better critics in the later part of the course. However, this explanation seems less plausible in light of results that will be presented in the next part of this chapter.

Associated with difficulties of interpretation are difficulties with the analysis. The biggest issue is that the analysis should control not only for the characteristics of the person being rated but also for the characteristics of the individual who filled out the instrument. This requires specific statistical expertise; therefore, the analysis may not be practical for evaluating adaptive performance on a routine basis in a wide range of courses in the future.

The difficulty of interpreting the data, and difficulties with implementing the instruments and analyzing the data, led us to conclude that peer evaluations will not be a good approach for future assessments of AWALP. We therefore decided to eliminate it as a measure for the remaining two classes.

Student and Guide Ratings of Teams

The training effectiveness outcomes we have reviewed thus far address adaptive performance at the individual level. We also developed a measure to assess adaptability at the team level for practical exercises, using both the students and guides as raters. The measure required participants to rate whether the dimensions of adaptive performance were required in each exercise and to rate the team's effectiveness on these dimensions.

We sought to answer the following questions about ratings of adaptability within teams:

- Regarding requirements, do students
  - recognize the dimensions of adaptive performance tapped in course activities?
  - become more accurate in their judgments over time?
- Regarding performance, do students and guides
  - rate teams favorably with regard to behaviors associated with relevant dimensions of adaptive performance in the exercises?
  - agree in ratings of team performance?
  - improve in agreement about performance ratings over time?[5]

---

[5]   We also intended to assess whether students had shared mental models of their team's performance and whether agreement in students' ratings increased over time. We calculated intraclass correlations (ICCs) for team ratings, but because students tended to have limited variation in ratings, with most ratings ranging from 4 to 6, ICCs appear very low. Thus, the ICCs do not provide a good indicator of within-group agreement.

While a key interest is whether the students and guides generally agree in their ratings of the teams, we also addressed the question of whether team performance improved over time (from day 3 to day 7), particularly based on data from the course guides (we might expect generally high and less-variable ratings from students, as we observed with peer ratings and as described in the previous section).

Method

We developed a rating form consisting of 15 items addressing six of the adaptive performance dimensions: creative thinking, dealing with ambiguity, interpersonal adaptability, cultural adaptability, decision-making under stress, and physical adaptability (see Table 4.1). Most of the items were abbreviated versions of the items used to assess attitudes

Table 4.1
Dimensions and Items for Measures of Team Adaptability

Dimension	Label	Item
Physical	Phy	Use physical strength or agility
Interpersonal	Int1	Encourage input from other members
	Int2	Modify one's behavior to get along with others
	Int3	Consider others' viewpoints
	Int4	Read others' nonverbal cues
Ambiguity	Am1	Make decisions with incomplete information
	Am2	Adjust actions rapidly to changes in the situation
Cultural	Cul1	Interact with others who have different values and customs
	Cul2	Learn rules for appropriate interaction with different social groups
Creative thinking	Cre1	Look at problems from different angles
	Cre2	Develop innovative ideas
Decisionmaking under stress	Str1	Quickly analyze options
	Str2	Remain calm under pressure
	Str3	Make decisions with limited time
Planning	Plan	Plan a strategy for performing the task in advance

toward adaptive performance reported in Chapter Three. Thus, items were only indirectly related to dimensions, with no specific mention of the dimension itself. For example, "Encouraging input from other team members" related to the interpersonal dimension, and "Looking at problems from different angles" related to the creative thinking dimension. We did not include items assessing learning tasks, technologies, and procedures because we expected that it would be difficult to observe whether others engage in this behavior. At the recommendation of the guides, we also included an item assessing planning behavior, given its importance in fostering shared mental models. With the exception of physical adaptability and planning, which had one item each, there were two to four items for each dimension.

Participants were asked to complete the rating form after team exercises on three days of the course: day 3 ("Firepoint"), day 5 ("Starburst,"), and day 7 ("Engage the Population"). Like other practical exercises in the course, these exercises involve solving problems or making judgments for which teams, on average, will outperform individuals (McGrath, 1984). The exercises included ambiguous conditions or information, as well as "curveballs"—unforeseen events or conditions designed to induce stress, require creative thinking, and mandate a change in plans. One of the important lessons from several of the tasks in these exercises is that students will perform more effectively if they share information and collaborate than if they attempt to complete the tasks alone. The "Firepoint" exercise involves combat casualty care and extraction. Students are organized into eight- to nine-person teams and must perform a variety of tasks that require division of labor, problem solving, team decisionmaking, and physical strength and coordination that exceed the capabilities of individual members. The "Starburst" exercise is a complex capstone exercise for the first half of the course that involves a counterinsurgency environment. Students are organized into nine- to 13-person teams. The exercise starts with a land navigation event requiring a variety of problem-solving tasks. Later, each team must plan, prepare, and execute a mission; one team has a patrolling and quick-reaction force mission; one has a personal security detail mission; and one has an opposing force mission. The "Engage the Population" exercise challenges teams to deal with ambiguity in a real urban environment. Students are organized into eight- to nine-person teams and are instructed to collect information of value to a commander preparing to conduct military operations in the city. Students are told to consider areas, structures, capabilities, organizations, people, and events (ASCOPE) or political, military, economic, social, infrastructure, information, physical environment, and time (PMESII-PT) variables, but otherwise, instructions on the commander's intent are ambiguous. At the end of the exercise, each team is required to prepare and deliver a report to a senior military officer.

Students were instructed to write a code at the top of the form that would enable us to match their responses across exercises while maintaining their anonymity. Then, for each item on the form, students were asked to first rate whether the exercise required the behavior using a three-point scale (i.e., "not at all or limited requirements," "some requirements," or "substantial requirements"). Next, they were asked to rate whether their team as a whole performed effectively on the behavior using a six-point scale ranging from "strongly disagree" to "strongly agree." Students completed the rating form independently.

For ratings of the requirements for each behavior, the guides consulted with each other to determine one set of judgments that constituted the "right answer." For ratings of effectiveness, guides independently rated the teams that they accompanied during the exercise.

Results for Requirements

Average ratings were calculated at the team level. Figures 4.3 through 4.5 show the average requirement ratings for the 15 items in each of the three exercises. Although the items were presented in a random order on the survey form, they are grouped by adaptive performance dimension in the figures to facilitate interpretation of results.

The similarity between students' and guides' ratings of requirements for adaptive performance generally varied across the three exercises. We considered a difference between students' average ratings and the "correct" answer of 0.5 or greater to be "large." As shown in Figures 4.3 and 4.4, students failed to recognize that some adaptive performance dimensions were not relevant to the Firepoint and Starburst exercises. In contrast, as shown in Figure 4.5, students recognized

Figure 4.3
Student and Guide Ratings of Firepoint Requirements, Day 3

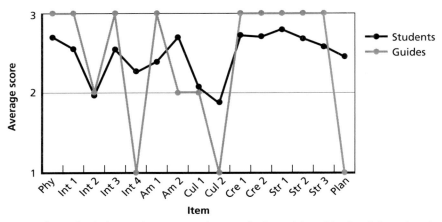

NOTE: Phy = physical, Int = interpersonal, Am = dealing with ambiguity, Cul = cultural,
Str = decisionmaking under stress, Plan = planning.
RAND RR504-4.3

Figure 4.4
Student and Guide Ratings of Starburst Requirements, Day 5

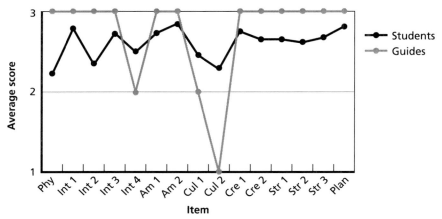

RAND RR504-4.4

that Engage the Population did not require physical adaptability, suggesting that they were starting to discriminate between dimensions of
adaptive performance that were and were not required. However, there

Figure 4.5
Student and Guide Ratings of Engage the Population Requirements, Day 7

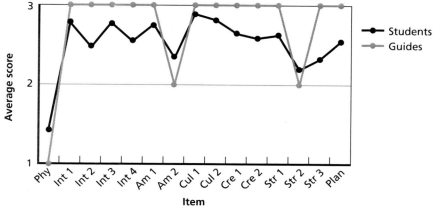

RAND *RR504-4.5*

were also large discrepancies between student and guide ratings for two or more other items in each exercise.[6]

Students appeared to become more accurate in their ratings over time. As shown in Figures 4.3 through 4.5, the number of items with large discrepancies decreased from five in Firepoint to four in Starburst and two in Engage the Population. In addition, on average, the absolute value of the discrepancies between students and guide ratings decreased over time, from 0.51 in Firepoint to 0.43 in Starburst and 0.35 in Engage the Population. These results could, however, also reflect a general lack of variability in students' ratings, coupled with lower variability in guides' ratings for Starburst and Engage the Population than for Firepoint.

---

[6]   In Firepoint, these included the two items about dealing with ambiguity, "Make decisions with incomplete information," and "Adjust actions rapidly to change in the situation." In Starburst, these included physical adaptability and two items assessing interpersonal adaptability ("Modify one's behavior to get along with others" [Int2] and "Read others' nonverbal cues" [Int4]). In Engage the Population, these included one of the same interpersonal adaptability items (Int2) and an item assessing decisionmaking under stress ("Make decisions with limited time" [Str3]).

Results for Performance

Results for performance are shown in Figures 4.6 through 4.9. Figure 4.6 shows the results aggregated across all three exercises, and Figures 4.7 through 4.9 show the results for the individual exercises. Note that guides were told not to rate performance for items with "not at all or limited requirements" ratings, which is the reason for gaps in the guides' performance ratings.

In general, both students and guides gave favorable ratings of team performance. In general, students' average scores hovered around 5, corresponding to an "agree" response, and most of the guides' ratings ranged from approximately 4 (i.e., "agree somewhat") to 5, although average scores were below 4, toward the "somewhat disagree" range for a few of the items (Figure 4.8).

However, students consistently rated team performance more favorably than guides did. At the item level across exercises, discrepancies between guides' and students' ratings were particularly large for three of the items: "Adjusting actions rapidly to changes in the situation" (ambiguity [Am2] in Figure 4.6)), "Developing innovative ideas" (creative thinking [Cre2]), and "Quickly analyzing options" (decision-

Figure 4.6
Student and Guide Ratings of Team Performance Effectiveness at Item Level, Aggregated Across Exercises

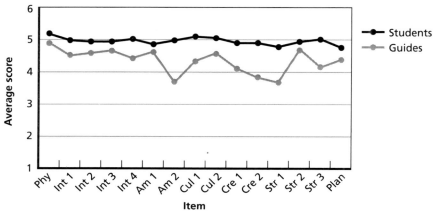

Figure 4.7
Student and Guide Ratings of Team Performance on Firepoint

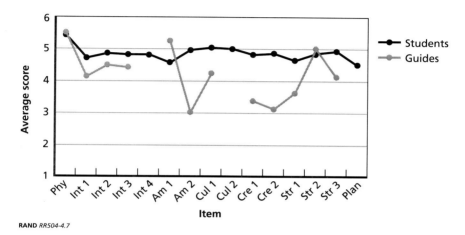

RAND RR504-4.7

Figure 4.8
Student and Guide Ratings of Team Performance on Starburst

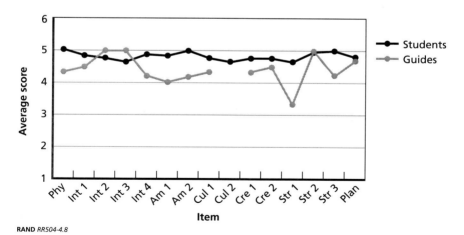

RAND RR504-4.8

making under stress [Str1]). Differences between guides' and students' ratings also were statistically significant for "Reading others' nonverbal cues" (interpersonal [Int4]), "Looking at problems from different angles" (creative thinking [Cre1]), "Making decisions with limited

Figure 4.9
Student and Guide Ratings of Team Performance on Engage the Population

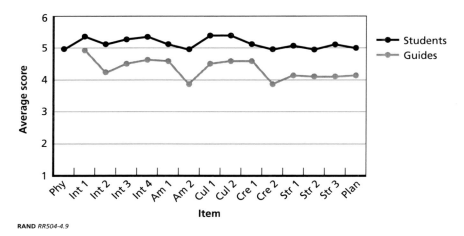

time" (decisionmaking under stress [Str3]), and "Planning a strategy for performing the task in advance" (Plan).

As might be expected given the differences in their experience levels, **students generally discriminated less than guides did in rating team effectiveness across the different dimensions of adaptive performance**. Figure 4.6 shows that, in comparison to guides, students' ratings were more similar across the items, as indicated by the relatively flatter slope for student ratings. Similar patterns are also evident in the individual exercises shown in Figures 4.7 through 4.9. While these ratings might reflect students' true opinions, the result could indicate a tendency not to think too much about the questions before responding, a possibility that is supported by anecdotal information from guides about how quickly students sometimes completed the forms. However, it is interesting to note that, in Engage the Population, the up-and-down pattern of students' ratings more closely mirrors that of the guides' ratings (Figure 4.9).

At the same time, students also perceived that team effectiveness was increasing by the third exercise, a view that the guides did not necessarily share. Figure 4.10 depicts the average effectiveness scores across the items in each of the three exercises. Note the relatively flat slope for

Figure 4.10
Student and Guide Performance Ratings at Exercise Level Aggregated Across Items

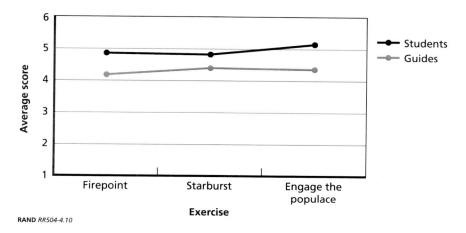

guides' ratings (although given the increasing difficulty of the exercises over time, the relative constancy in guides' ratings could suggest that teams were improving in adaptive performance). In contrast, the students' ratings increased from the first to the third exercise.

Differences between students and guides in views of team effectiveness are also apparent in results for the individual exercises shown in Figures 4.7 through 4.9. In Firepoint and Starburst, there is some "crossover" between student and guide ratings, such that students gave their teams higher ratings on some dimensions and guides gave teams higher ratings on others. However, in Engage the Population, students gave their teams higher ratings than guides did on *all* the items. **Thus, students' ratings of effectiveness changed over time, but they appeared to become more confident (or overconfident) about the level of adaptability in their teams by the end of the course.**

While the preceding figures show results for the three AWALP classes as a whole, student and guide ratings also can be calculated for individual teams. For example, Figure 4.11 shows differences between guide and student effectiveness ratings for one of the teams in Firepoint. (Ratings are shown only for required behaviors as determined

Figure 4.11
Student and Guide Performance Ratings for a Single Team, Firepoint

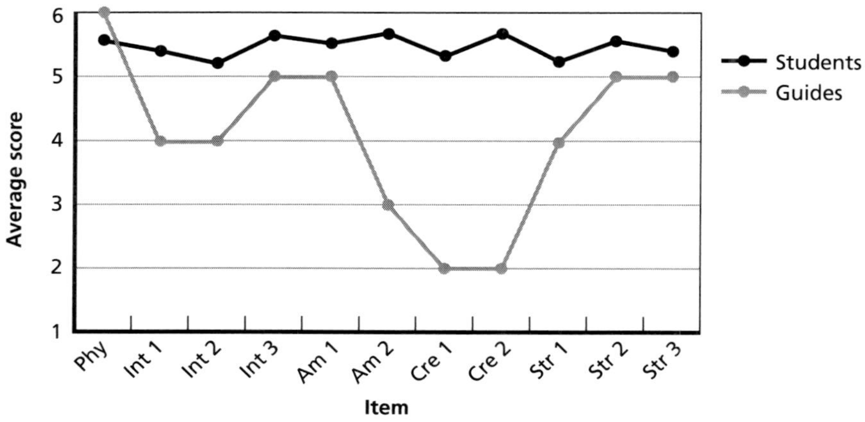

by the guides.) In Chapter Six, we discuss ways in which these ratings could be used to support AARs in the course.

Finally, there was quite a bit of variability among some of the guides in rating team performance effectiveness. Some guides tended to give low ratings (1s and 2s) to the teams that they observed, while other guides gave their teams higher ratings (from 3 to 6) on the same criteria. Guides were evaluating different teams, so it is possible that the lower ratings accurately reflect team performance. However, given that a subset of the guides provided the lower ratings, it is also possible that there are systematic differences in how guides are assessing performance, which in turn might affect feedback to the teams. In Chapter Six, we propose a strategy to assess and improve consistency among guides in evaluating performance.

Conclusions

This chapter showed clear evidence of increased cognitive learning associated with AWALP. Results showed substantial improvement in declarative knowledge of adaptive performance concepts and showed that learning occurred regardless of students' general cognitive ability or education. Team ratings of requirements showed that students were generally accurate in identifying the adaptability behaviors required in practical exercises and that the accuracy of their judgments appeared to improve over time.

With regard to ratings of performance, both the guides and the students agreed that teams performed at least somewhat effectively across most adaptive performance dimensions, even as exercises became more complex and demanding. Guides' ratings, although relatively constant over time, may indicate behavioral learning, given that the exercises were increasing in difficulty. However, students generally discriminated less among different dimensions of adaptive performance. Students also tended to inflate ratings of team effectiveness relative to guides' ratings, and these discrepancies did not improve over time.

This chapter also featured an example of how we modified our evaluation approach during the study. Results of the peer evaluation showed uniformly high ratings given to peers in all areas of adaptive performance addressed and showed limited changes over time. Because of difficulties of interpretation, implementation, and analysis, we discontinued use of peer evaluations after the first class, and we recommend forgoing use of peer evaluations in further evaluations of AWALP.

CHAPTER FIVE

Results: Application of AWALP Principles on the Job and Longer-Term Attitudes Toward AWALP

This chapter addresses payoffs of AWALP to the Army in terms of graduates' application of adaptive performance principles on the job. We conducted telephone interviews with students and their supervisors to assess the longer term impact of AWALP on adaptive performance and attitudes after students returned to their units.

Purpose of Interviews

We interviewed both AWALP graduates and their supervisors three months and six months after the course ended. There were two primary goals. The first goal was to contribute to an understanding of how AWALP affects participants' work when they return to their units. The central question was whether the graduates have changed professionally as a result of the AWALP training, We addressed changes in professional conduct through questions about mentoring and training subordinates, conducting AARs and briefings, delegating tasks, and seeking input from others. The second goal was to understand whether participants' attitudes about the course changed once they returned to their units. We addressed attitudes through questions about recommending AWALP to others, needed course changes, and challenges to implementing AWALP principles. We also interviewed graduates' supervisors to learn their perspectives on how AWALP participants might have changed professionally as a result of the AWALP training.

Application of AWALP Principles and Attitudes Three Months Post-AWALP

Method and Response Rates

At the end of the Class 10 AWALP training in January 2013 and at the end of the Class 11 training in April 2013, we asked the graduates whether, in three months, they would be willing to participate in a brief telephone interview about their AWALP training experience. Of the 29 graduates in Class 10 (excluding operational advisors), 23 (64 percent) indicated they were willing to be interviewed.[1] Of the 35 graduates in Class 11, 17 (49 percent) indicated that they were willing to be interviewed. We first tried to contact graduates by email to request telephone interviews. However, because we had initially low responses from graduates from both classes, we turned to phone calls, which resulted in much greater success. From early April through early May 2013, we were able to contact and interview 13 graduates from Class 10. In August 2013, we were able to contact and interview 11 graduates from Class 11. Thus, in total, we were able to interview 24 out of 62 potentially willing participants, or 39 percent, across classes. Table 5.1 shows the response rates by class and overall. The 24 graduates we interviewed represented the full range of ranks in the courses: 8 percent were E5; 33 percent were E6; 25 percent were E7; 17 percent were E8-9; and the remaining 17 percent were commissioned officers.

Table 5.1
AWALP Graduate Interview Response Rates, by Class

	Class 10	Class 11	Overall
Total in class	27[a]	35	62
Willing to be interviewed	23	17	40
Total interviewed	13	11	24
Response rate (%)	48	31	39

[a] Excludes the nine operational advisors who had taken AWALP before.

---

[1]   As noted in Chapter Two, nine students were taking the course a second time as part of their operational advisor training. We excluded these students from our analysis of application of course principles on the job.

The three-month follow-up interviews took 10 to 20 minutes each. Each followed a semistructured interview protocol. We asked interviewees about whether they altered the way they engaged in a number of adaptability behaviors reflecting the "leader practice" items reported in Chapter Three (see Table 5.2), with prompts on various topics if interviewees did not address them. If interviewees reported having changed their behaviors, we asked for examples. We also asked interviewees who in the organization was most affected by the changes. Finally, we asked about graduates' attitudes in three areas: whether they (1) would recommend the AWALP to others, (2) saw the need for changes in the course, and (3) perceived any obstacles in implementing the principles they learned. Appendix D provides the interview questions.

Results: Report of Changes in Work Activities

Eighty-eight percent of graduates reported that they changed professionally as a result of AWALP. We asked graduates specifically about whether they had changed the way they coach, train, give AARs, brief commanding officers, delegate, and seek subordinate input. Table 5.2 shows the number of interviewees who responded by activity. Note that, because of interview time constraints or interviewee job

Table 5.2
Frequency of Changes in Work Activity Three Months After AWALP Graduation

Activity	Number of Graduates Reporting Changes
Coaching	16
Training	15
Delegating	15
Seeking and using subordinate input	15
Conducting AARs	10
Briefing commanding officers	3

functions, we did not ask every graduate about every activity. There-fore, these numbers should be understood as only rough estimates of the total of each kind of change.

We discuss the changes reported for each activity more specifi-cally in the following subsections, starting with those activities that were mentioned most often.

Coaching

The majority of graduates provided specific examples to demon-strate how they have modified the way they coach and mentor sub-ordinates. A common theme was that post-AWALP, graduates realized the value of spending more time on thoughtful conversation with, and listening to, their soldiers and on how such processes can foster better solutions to problems. One graduate described how AWALP made him feel more empowered and how he wanted to pass that feeling on to his subordinates by increasing how much he back-briefs his soldiers and discusses intent, pitfalls, and choices about what to change for next time. Another graduate explained:

> I used to say "this is how you're going to learn this, OK, no ques-tions, good," but now I take time with the training, have my sol-diers ask me questions, and before I know it, they know how to use and operate the machinery.

Other graduates report "listening to complaints rather than blow-ing them off," "emphasizing why" to approach tasks in certain ways, and being more patient and encouraging subordinates to "figure things out rather than just doing it this way."

Training

The majority of graduates provided specific examples of how AWALP has affected the way they themselves conduct training within their units. Most frequently, graduates mentioned ways they have been able to use what they learned during AWALP to improve how they conduct physical training (PT) and range work. For exam-ple, two graduates (from the same unit) used AWALP concepts to create and implement a PT workout that included land navigation, counter–improvised explosive device, other team exercises, and getting through obstacles. Two other graduates had their respective soldiers work in teams as part of land navigation exercises and said that what they learned in AWALP helped them develop and manage the exercises. Likewise, Roselle, 2013, found that even one month after graduation, AWALP participants had begun to incorporate adaptive performance principles into existing training.

Several graduates have also been very pleased with the results of following the AWALP method of range instruction, which empowers participants to analyze their own marksmanship data and make decisions on how to alter their approach. For example, one graduate explained that, post-AWALP, he did primary military instruction "for soldiers who normally wouldn't do so well and they all scored in the 30s." Another says that he has been following AWALP shooting procedures, teaching his soldiers exactly what AWALP taught him, and his soldiers "have absolutely improved their gunnery scores."

Most graduates reported that they had not had much opportunity to integrate AWALP principles into how they conduct other types of training, including training intended to promote effective teamwork, or to improve complex problem solving or technical skills and procedures (other than shooting). There were, however, a few exceptions. A few graduates reported using AWALP principles to help their soldiers problem-solve, work more effectively in teams, and prepare for ambiguous situations. One graduate responded that, pre-AWALP, in training on "Skill Level 1, ambush-type raids," he would typically repeat the same topics because he thought that soldiers learn best through repetition. Based on what he learned in AWALP, however, he is now trying to incorporate more variety and ambiguity into this type of training.

A few graduates explained at three months posttraining that they had not yet had the opportunity to integrate AWALP principles into training but have thought about how they will when they have the opportunity. One graduate had plans to use one of the AWALP exercises a few months down the road. He explained that, when he has the opportunity, he will break his soldiers into teams (keeping like ranks together so that privates can lead their peers) and present surprise challenges to each team.

Three graduates who reported not integrating AWALP principles into how they conduct training and who have no plans to do so in the future explained that they are not currently in a position to lead training.

Delegating
Most graduates responded that AWALP changed how they delegate, reflecting an outcomes-based approach. A common theme was graduates' conscious intention to delegate in a way that provided less procedural guidance and more clarity on the ultimate goal. One graduate summarized what he learned from AWALP as the following: "My way might be the way I'd do it, but let's see what happens with less guidance." Another graduate explained that, post-AWALP, his delegation style is to say, "Here's your mission, you've got the nuts and bolts, you build the motor the way you think it needs to be built, then we'll look at it and tweak it." Another explained that, before AWALP, if the subordinate "didn't get it right the first time, [he would] just do it himself. . . . But AWALP said, don't give them the answers, make them do the work." Thus, since AWALP, he has been following that principle. A third graduate applied AWALP delegation principles to how he organizes his unit, such that the more experienced soldiers now mentor those newer to the unit. Likewise, Roselle, 2013, also identified a theme among graduates that they were more prone to empower team members to find their own solutions to issues that arose in training.

Not everyone with subordinates completely embraced AWALP principles. For example, one graduate seemed to continue to provide quite strict procedural guidance but did provide more clarity on the ultimate goal, explaining that he now says to his subordinates "do it in this manner and this is why I want you to do it in that manner."

Even graduates without direct managing responsibility for subordinates reported that they were applying AWALP delegation principles to their work in some way. One described how he now more frequently looks to others' expertise to help with project-based work. Another, describing himself as a "worker bee" with little opportunity to delegate, explained that, during the Advanced Leader Course, he did very well on a delegating exercise because of what he learned in AWALP.

Five graduates indicated that AWALP did not change their delegation style. Three graduates responded that they had no opportunity to delegate, and thus, AWALP had no impact on them for this skill; two said that they already delegated per AWALP principles before the training.

Seeking and Using Subordinate Input

Graduates' responses to whether their AWALP training experience affected how they seek and use input from subordinates varied and can be understood on a continuum. The majority responded that they learned in AWALP that subordinates can have good ideas and that graduates can now ask subordinates for more input. Several graduates explained that they have always asked for input from subordinates, but AWALP strengthened the habit. One explained that he always asked subordinates for input; however, he explained that AWALP changed his rationale for doing so. Specifically, pre-AWALP, he realized the benefit of learning from substantive experts about a given topic area. Post-AWALP, he began asking for input as a relationship-building strategy. Roselle, 2013, also found that graduates reported encouraging input from team members to a greater degree after completing AWALP training.

Finally, three graduates explained that they have always asked for input and that, in this regard, AWALP training did not affect their professional work.

Conducting AARs

Fewer than half of the graduates responded that AWALP affected the way they conduct AARs. However, most respondents shared the sentiment that the AWALP method is more useful than the traditional "three improvement, three sustainment" model that has been the Army status quo. While the goal of AARs is to understand what happened in an event, why it happened, and how it could be done better, sometimes these reviews become simplified to the point that they become little more than short lists of what was done well and what needs to improve. In contrast, in AWALP, an AAR is a significant learning process that encourages critical thinking, reflection, and discussion among all those who participated in the event. Comments from graduates showed that they were applying this approach to AARs on the job. For example, one graduate explained that he now asks his subordinates, "What was your intent today? How did you achieve it? Tell me about the end state." Several others mentioned moving away from the "three up, three down" model to asking soldiers to talk about what they did, how they felt they did, what could have improved the activity, and what could have been a better course of action.

Few graduates mentioned trying to influence their peers' or commanders' AAR style. However, three graduates mentioned an intention to share principles about conducting AARs learned in AWALP with others in their units in addition to their subordinates.

For the most part, the graduates who had not changed the way their approach to AARs explained that they had not yet had the opportunity to conduct AARs. A small minority, including two with Special Forces backgrounds, said they already follow AWALP principles in giving AARs.

Briefing Commanding Officers
For the majority of graduates, their AWALP training did not change the way they brief commanding officers. Only three graduates provided examples of how the AWALP training affected how they briefed a commanding officer. One graduate explained that, post-AWALP, he now presents proposed solutions to problems as part of the briefing.

The remaining graduates, however, responded that AWALP did not change how they brief a commanding officer or that they have not had an opportunity to brief at all. Four graduates said that AWALP did not affect how they brief commanding officers because they already follow AWALP principles to brief. One explained that he was also required to brief commanding officers in "the formal way."

Results: Use of Outcomes-Based Strategies for Training, Delegating, and Mentoring
While graduates did not say so directly, some of the examples above demonstrate the use of outcomes-based strategies in leading others. We also reviewed interview transcripts more holistically to analyze how

much AWALP seems to affect graduates' use of outcomes-based strategies more broadly. **Of the 24 three-month interviewees, 11 clearly expressed ideas that suggested AWALP influenced their use of outcomes-based strategies.** Some of the quotes above reflect this change. The following is another representative quote:

> AWALP has impacted everything from the way I give instructions at the beginning of training through the AAR. I'm more concerned about outcomes and having subordinates think about the process and solutions. I now encourage more thinking rather than the old way of telling them how to do each step.

Eight graduates seemed to loosely express a shift toward increased use of outcomes-based strategies. For example,

> I have soldiers think more for themselves.

> Now I use a really hands-off approach, and if they get off track, I try to coach them back.

> I have a lot of newly promoted sergeants; I'm delegating a little more to the new guys, having the old guys mentor the new guys.

Only five graduates did not express any ideas related to an outcomes approach.

Results: Who Is Most Affected by Graduates' Changes

Graduates' responses to questions about coaching, training, delegating, and seeking input demonstrate that nearly all AWALP graduates—20 of 24 interviewed—feel that they have been able to integrate AWALP principles into their work with subordinates in some way. Direct comments about subordinates' reactions to AWALP principles include, "Subordinates have been very receptive" and "they feel my trust, confidence in them."

Seven graduates reported also attempting to share AWALP principles with their peers, including three who are working with a particularly receptive unit that has sent a number of leaders to AWALP trainings. For example, one said "I am trying to show other platoon leaders how well AWALP principles can work with his [sic] platoon."

Four graduates mentioned that they have also been able to have some impact on the unit through sharing AWALP principles with their commanders. One graduate responded that command climate and leadership has been comfortable with, and supportive of, integrating AWALP principles into unit practices. Another noted the effect on his unit, but qualified his response, believing AWALP principles have spread "all the way up to the company level but not beyond that."

Finally, four graduates' comments suggested that they had not successfully spread AWALP principles to others (subordinates, peers, or the unit) on return from the training. One respondent explained that he is the "new guy in the unit, so it's hard for others to recognize changes in [his] work behavior." Another said that no one recognizes any changes in his professional work because of the nature of his job.

As we describe below, a number of other graduates seem to be implementing AWALP principles with their subordinates, yet they also cited command climate and leadership buy-in as challenges to fully implementing AWALP principles.

Results: Changes in Attitudes

We asked three questions that addressed graduates' attitudes toward AWALP three months after training and compared these responses with those reported at the end of AWALP. These comparisons are discussed below. **Overall, answers to each of the three questions remained relatively constant on day 10 of training and three months later.**

Recommending AWALP Training to Others

Graduates' attitudes about recommending AWALP training to others remained highly favorable three months after the course. As noted in Chapter Three, at the end of training, all students reported that they would recommend AWALP to others. Three months after the training, every graduate also responded that he would—and in many cases has—recommended AWALP to others. One said that he has been recommending AWALP ever since he returned, and another echoed that, saying he tells everyone to go to the course because "it will change how you think about and do things." Another said that AWALP should be required when soldiers become NCOs.

Recommendations to Improve AWALP Training

The nature of recommendations for improving AWALP training also did not change markedly between the end of the course and the three-month interviews. At the end of the course, more than one-half of the graduates suggested a change, and three months after AWALP, nine of 24 graduates suggested a change. Fifteen graduates said they had no recommendations because they believe that all aspects of the AWALP training should stay as they are. Of the nine graduates who offered a recommendation for change, only one made a critical comment; he thought that the training should be "tighter" because he felt that the more junior attendees were "seeing it as play time." The other eight made a variety of more positive suggestions; these included that more people should have to go through the AWALP training, that the training should be longer in terms of days, that more range time would be useful, and that more "chaos" in the exercises would be useful. Another graduate commented on the usefulness of not restricting AWALP activities according to rank. He explained that he "got a lot out of interacting with more senior soldiers," such that now he understands majors and higher-level officers better, which helps in learning how to interact with them, including asking for permission to implement AWALP principles.

Challenges to Implementing AWALP Principles

Similarly, graduates continued to report command climate and leadership as the chief obstacles to implementing AWALP principles. The most commonly mentioned challenges related to entrenched attitudes, command climate, and "Armyisms," such as "old-school sergeant majors," and the "I-told-you-so mind-set." One graduate described the challenges of peers who are "stuck in their ways" and also of contractors at range control who limit how much he is permitted to alter range work to adapt AWALP strategies. Several other interviewees expressed concerns about the time and resources needed to implement AWALP principles, particularly for training.

Twelve of the graduates mentioned challenges in implementation. This is likely an underestimate of the number who actually saw challenges because we modified our interview protocol between the Class

10 and Class 11 interviews to ask more explicitly about challenges in the second round. Consequently, Class 11 graduates were more specific about challenges they had encountered than were Class 10 graduates.

Other Feedback

The only feedback graduates offered beyond the structured interview protocol was their praise for the AWALP training. The comments they made included "Excellent"; "Great"; "Outstanding"; "One of my favorite courses"; "People were very professional; very wise, very engaged teachers"; and "The best [engagement skills training] I've ever been to, best ten days of instruction I've ever gotten out of the military, period—in over ten years." Two graduates made the point that AWALP makes young leaders more three dimensional by teaching them to plan, teach, and execute.

The two graduates with Special Forces backgrounds mentioned that AWALP did not impact the way they work in any of the areas above because they had already learned to incorporate adaptive performance principles into their work through their prior training.

Application of AWALP Principles and Attitudes Six Months Post-AWALP

Method

We followed up with the Class 10 graduates roughly six months after AWALP training, in August and September 2013. We engaged graduates in brief, five- to ten-minute conversations about whether they had been able to implement AWALP principles to any greater extent since we last spoke in April 2013. If they responded affirmatively, we asked what they had been able to do. If they responded negatively, we asked why. We were able to speak with ten of the 16 Class 10 graduates (63 percent).

Results

At six months after training, more than half the graduates reported that they were continuing to apply AWALP principles to

**their professional performance, particularly in how they delegate
to, and solicit advice from, subordinates and design new training.**
Interviews suggested that, six months after training, implementation
of AWALP principles had not increased from three months after the
course. However, three graduates who were implementing AWALP
principles at the three-month period indicated that they had changed
units and roles and had had little to no opportunity to implement
AWALP principles in their new positions. Finally, one graduate (who
had indicated some efforts at the three-month period) reported after six
months that finding the time to implement and actually remember the
AWALP principles had been major challenges.

Interviews of Supervisors

Method
We asked the Class 11 interviewees ($n = 11$) and the Class 10 interviewees with whom we followed up at six months after AWALP ($n = 10$)
whether we could conduct a brief telephone interview with their supervisors about ways in which graduates might have changed professionally as a result of the AWALP training. Asking graduates' permission
to talk with supervisors was used to comply with Institutional Review
Board requirements. No graduates refused to give us permission to talk
with their supervisors or were outwardly resistant to the request. However, we were successful in speaking with only four of the 21 supervisors we sought to interview. The following results should be interpreted
with caution, because the sample size was extremely small.[2]

---

[2] For nine of the 17 not interviewed, we ended up not asking for contact information.
In seven cases, all six months after AWALP, the graduate's supervisor had changed since
AWALP. Thus, the current supervisor would not be able to speak to a change in the graduate's performance from pre- to post-AWALP. In another case, the commander was overseas
and unreachable. Finally, we decided not to pursue one graduate because his commander
worked for AWG. For four of the 17 not interviewed, the graduate indicated a willingness to
provide contact information in the future or have the supervisor call us, but follow-ups were
unsuccessful. The remaining three graduates did provide supervisor contact information, but
we were unable to actually get in touch with the supervisor. Some of these numbers may not
have been reliable contact information.

We asked supervisors about their role in selecting students for AWALP, the criteria they used for selection, and how the graduates changed after completing AWALP.

Results

Each of the four supervisors we spoke with responded that they saw meaningful, positive changes in how the graduates conducted themselves professionally on returning from AWALP. The supervisors were most able to comment on their communication with the graduates and how the graduates planned training. The supervisors felt that graduates were more self-reliant and better at communicating logical thought processes. They also reported that graduates were designing training that would help develop AWALP principles in subordinates and were doing so in creative yet viable ways. Supervisors were generally not able to comment on how the graduates interacted with subordinates in terms of coaching, delegating, or soliciting input because they did not see these interactions. One supervisor explained that, for AWALP graduates to have an effect on their units posttraining, they must already have earned the "white space"—or respect—within the unit prior to going to the training.

Conclusions

Graduates reported substantial application of AWALP principles on the job after three months, especially in the areas of coaching, training, delegating to subordinates, and seeking subordinate input. Moreover, many graduates reported applying outcomes-based strategies for training, delegating, and mentoring, leaving more freedom for subordinates to address tasks and challenges. For most, these positive effects of AWALP were sustained six months after graduation. Reported changes were less common in other areas, such as conducting AARs and briefing commanding officers, although many of the graduates reported no opportunity to engage in these activities in their current roles. While AWALP principles were successfully disseminated to graduates' subordinates, dissemination was somewhat less successful to peers and commanders and throughout the unit. Results reflect some of the factors in the work environment that inhibit training transfer, such as insufficient opportunities to engage in newly learned skills on the job and an unsupportive organizational culture (Grossman and Salas, 2011; Rouiller and Goldstein, 1993; Salas et al., 2012).

Graduates also remained extremely positive about AWALP three months after the course. All graduates would still recommend the course to others, and few recommended course changes. However, graduates also saw the same potential obstacles to applying AWALP principles once back at their units, with command climate ("Army-isms") and entrenched leadership still the most frequently mentioned challenges.

Supervisors were likewise positive about the effect of AWALP on graduates' behavior after the course, particularly with respect to observing improvements in training planning and communications with the commanding officers. However, a much larger sample of supervisors is needed to draw meaningful conclusions about changes in graduates' behavior. Difficulties in recruiting supervisors likely occurred, in part, because the evaluation was a research study and therefore required graduates' consent to contact their supervisors, and we were not able to reach all graduates. This requirement would not be in effect when the Army conducts its own evaluations in the future. In Chapter Six, we discuss additional strategies to engage supervisors in follow-up discussions, as well as alternative measures of training transfer and impact.

CHAPTER SIX

Summary, Conclusions, and Recommendations

This chapter summarizes our results and draws conclusions based on the findings. We then present recommendations about AWALP instruction and about how the evaluation of AWALP could be improved in the future. We then broaden our discussion outside of the current course, addressing how the AWALP approach to adaptability training could be expanded in the Army. Finally, we describe how the methods used in this study might be applied to evaluating adaptability training in other contexts.

Summary of Key Findings and Conclusions from AWALP Evaluation

Table 6.1 summarizes key findings from the evaluation of AWALP. Results provide evidence of course success across a range of measures. The following sections discuss these findings in more depth.

Reactions
Surveys administered at the end of AWALP showed that students were extremely satisfied with the course structure, content, and delivery. In fact, students' reactions toward AWALP were much more favorable than those active-duty leaders expressed about institutional training in general in the 2013 CASAL survey (Riley et al., 2013). AWALP students attribute their learning largely to the content of the course and to the training methods, which differ substantially from typical Army training. All AWALP students would recommend the

Table 6.1
Summary of Key Findings

Outcomes	Key Findings
Reactions to AWALP	Students were extremely satisfied with the course structure, content, and delivery, attributing learning largely to course content (adaptive performance) and the training methods, which differ substantially from typical Army training.
Attitudes toward adaptive performance	There was substantial improvement in self-efficacy for and interest in being adaptable, even after accounting for students' individual characteristics associated with adaptive performance. Results suggest an increase in the perceived need for adaptive performance in the students' current jobs.
Knowledge about course concepts	Students showed increased knowledge of AWALP concepts. AWALP was successful at fostering knowledge gain for a wide range of students.
Team adaptive performance	Students' and guides' ratings of requirements for adaptive performance generally were similar to each other across the three exercises. Evidence for improved student accuracy in ratings of requirements over time was mixed. Both students and guides gave favorable ratings of team performance, but students seemed to become more confident about the level of team adaptive performance as the course progressed.
Application of AWALP principles on the job; attitudes over time	Students reported substantial application of AWALP principles, especially in coaching, training, delegating to subordinates, and seeking subordinate input. While AWALP principles were successfully disseminated to graduates' subordinates, dissemination was somewhat less successful to peers and commanders and throughout the unit. Graduates remained positive about AWALP training but found command climate and entrenched leadership the biggest obstacles to applying AWALP principles. Graduates' supervisors were positive about effect of AWALP on graduates, but interpreting results requires caution because the sample size was small.

course to others. Very few students noted any weaknesses with the course, and of those students who provided recommendations, most gave suggestions aimed at enhancing a course that they already felt was effective. In addition, interviews of course graduates showed that reactions remained favorable over time, although graduates faced challenges in applying the principles they learned in AWALP in Army units.

Changes in Learners

Changes in learners were evident in several outcome measures of attitudes and knowledge. Analysis of pretraining and posttraining survey responses showed large changes in self-efficacy, indicating that students felt more capable in all dimensions of adaptive performance and in putting adaptability concepts into leader practice. These findings converge with results of prior AWALP course evaluations, in which students reported being more prepared to be adaptable as a result of the course (see Chapter Two), but the current results are less subject to demand characteristics and do not show ceiling effects. Likewise, the current evaluation found that students were more interested in being adaptable in their jobs and in encouraging adaptability in the teams they lead. Moreover, improvements in self-efficacy and interest were substantial even after accounting for individual characteristics associated with adaptive performance. Results suggest that students' perceptions of their current jobs also changed, as they recognized a greater need for adaptability in their roles with respect to all the adaptability dimensions and most of the leader behaviors assessed.

Changes in learners were also evident in terms of greater knowledge of course material. Analysis of pretests and posttests showed substantial increase in declarative knowledge of AWALP concepts. This improvement was independent of students' general cognitive ability or education.

Evidence of learning was more mixed in ratings of team behavior. Students were generally accurate in rating the requirements for adaptive performance in team exercises, in which accuracy corresponded to guides' ratings. The accuracy of students' judgments of adaptability requirements appeared to have improved over time, although this result could also reflect decreasing variability in guides' ratings, corresponding to relatively "flat" student ratings across the exercises. In rating performance, both the guides and the students agreed that teams performed at least somewhat effectively across most adaptive performance dimensions, even as exercises became more complex and demanding. Consistent ratings of performance from guides on exercises with increasing levels of difficulty could indicate behavioral learning. However, students tended to inflate ratings of team effectiveness relative to guides' ratings, and these discrepancies did not improve over time (and, indeed, were most extreme at the end of the course).

Application of AWALP Principles on the Job

Results of interviews indicate substantial professional change in graduates after three months, especially in the areas of coaching, training, delegating to subordinates, and seeking subordinate input. Graduates' responses also demonstrated application of outcomes-based strategies on the job. For most respondents, positive effects of AWALP were sustained six months after graduation. Reported changes were less common in some areas, such as conducting AARs and briefing commanding officers, largely because graduates reported limited opportunities to engage in these activities in their current roles.

AWALP principles were disseminated most successfully to graduates' subordinates. Less success was reported in disseminating principles to peers and commanders and throughout the unit. These findings appear to be consistent with students' expectations about challenges in applying AWALP principles on the job; at the end of the course, students most often anticipated that leader buy-in and command climate would pose obstacles to implementation. Three months after returning to their jobs, graduates again identified leadership and climate as the principal impediments. Although the supervisors we talked with were positive about the effect of AWALP on graduates' behavior after the course, results should be interpreted with caution because of the extremely small sample size.

Improving AWALP

Overall, results showed only limited need for improvement in AWALP. The following subsections summarize and discuss possible modifications to the course.

Address Challenges to Implementing Adaptive Performance Concepts on the Job

On the last day of AWALP, students create training plans to implement once they return to their units. This activity encourages students to consider the realities of applying adaptability concepts in their jobs. As shown in the posttraining surveys, students anticipated that leader buy-in and command climate would be key challenges to implementing adaptive performance principles, and indeed, these were the predominant challenges graduates reported after returning to their jobs. Over time, we expect that receptivity to adaptability concepts will improve as a critical mass of soldiers participates in the course or learns about adaptability in other Army training. In the meantime, however, we recommend explicitly discussing in AWALP these potential obstacles and strategies to address them. After AWALP, creating a community of practice among graduates, with access to an online forum, can provide ongoing support by enabling leaders to share experiences and best practices. This approach has been successful in fostering tactical knowledge acquisition among Stryker brigade teams (Hallmark and Gayton, 2011).

Provide More Feedback to Students

Although students generally were satisfied with the feedback that guides provided, using the team rating instrument (at the end of Chapter Four) within an AAR could further enhance feedback and might foster convergence of students' and guides' ratings, which remained discrepant on day 7 of the course, and could contribute to enhanced team interaction and performance (Zaccaro et al., 2009). However, because sharing of guides' ratings with the students may be viewed as inconsistent with a constructivist instructional approach, which emphasizes learning through self-awareness, the students could be shown only their own team's ratings; the guides' ratings could be kept for their own use in the AAR or presented only after the AAR.

There are several ways that the ratings could be valuable, even if only the students' ratings are used. First, students' ratings could point to topics that are particularly important for guides to probe in the AAR (e.g., where there are large discrepancies between students' ratings and the guide's judgment), and the form's structure can ensure that important topics are not missed in the discussion. Second, displaying the average of students' ratings for each team, as well as variation within teams, could be the impetus for discussion in the AAR. For example, guides might use the results to inquire why students thought they did particularly well or poorly in particular adaptive performance dimensions. Or, considerable disagreement among students in ratings of some dimensions (some rate the team high, and others rate it low) could indicate that the team does not have a shared mental model; guides therefore might ask the students to discuss their positions to encourage building a common frame of reference. Third, asking students to complete the team rating form *before* and *after* the AAR (rather than just before) might also increase convergence of subsequent ratings by encouraging students to reflect more deeply on their performance. Reviewing students' pre-AAR and post-AAR ratings could reveal whether students are assimilating performance feedback.

AWG should also ensure that guides use the team rating forms consistently. Reliability among guides can be assessed by having multiple guides independently rate the same team during practical exercises or in practice sessions using observations of video recordings of the teams.

Guide ratings of students' individual effectiveness could be another source of feedback. We discuss this topic in the section on future evaluation of AWALP later in this chapter.

Update and Expand on Instruction of Team Adaptability

The Pulakos et al., 2000, taxonomy used as a basis for AWALP is a model of individual adaptive performance. However, the AWALP curriculum emphasizes performance in teams. While some of the Pulakos et al., 2000, dimensions of adaptive performance may be relevant to teams, Baard, Rench, and Kozlowski, 2014, argues that there may be additional dimensions of team adaptive performance that have not yet been identified. In addition, model development since the inception of AWALP has advanced the theory of team adaptation and related constructs. One notable example is Burke, Stagl, et al., 2006, which posits an input-throughput-output model of team adaptation in which individuals coming together as a team develop team processes for behavioral results (i.e., team actions), resulting in team adaptation (i.e., team innovation or modification), as reflected by new or modified structures, capacities, or actions. Inputs consist of individual and job characteristics. Throughputs consist of (1) four phases of team adaptability (situation assessment, plan formulation, plan execution, and team learning); (2) emergent cognitive and attitudinal states (shared mental models, team situation awareness, and psychological safety—the shared belief that the team is safe for risk taking); and (3) cognitive processes (e.g., cue recognition, including recognition of the need to adapt) and interpersonal processes (mutual monitoring, communication, backup behavior, and leadership), through which the four phases are enacted. While AWALP already addresses most of the factors in the Burke et al. model, the curriculum could be enhanced by reinforcing concepts, including planning, which entails determining a course of action, setting goals, and identifying members' roles and responsibilities; mutual monitoring, whereby team members observe one another in an attempt to catch and correct errors or slips in a timely way; and backup behavior, when team members help others who are having difficulty meeting their goals. The Burke et al. model may also be useful in AWALP as a way to provide instruction about the relationships among the inputs, throughputs and outcomes.[1]

Enhance Instruction of Adaptive Performance Dimensions

The evaluation results suggest that some fine-tuning of course content may enhance outcomes for a few of the adaptive performance dimensions. For example, some variation in responses about learning to handle ambiguous situations suggests that instruction in this area might be strengthened. Students reported significantly greater self-efficacy for this dimension of adaptive performance; however, guides' ratings of performance effectiveness for one aspect of dealing with ambiguity in

---

[1] Some of the concepts of the Burke et al. model, such as psychological safety, may be more applicable to teams with enduring membership; in AWALP, as in the Army more generally, team composition changes frequently. Thus, it would be important to identify potential boundary conditions of the Burke et al. model for Army teams, the impact of these conditions, and strategies to overcome their possible constraints on team adaptability.

teams—adjusting actions rapidly to changes in the situation—tended to be quite a bit lower than students' self-ratings. In addition, guides' ratings of team effectiveness in generating innovative ideas—which is one aspect of thinking creatively—suggest that this aspect of the course could be enhanced. While the course already included a number of practical exercises that call for innovative thinking, it could be useful to incorporate structured brainstorming techniques, such as brainwriting (Paulus and Yang, 2000), in which group members exchange written ideas in a round-robin fashion. AWG would need to determine the extent to which these areas are problematic and whether they can be addressed with modifications to the course. At the same time, adaptability, while malleable, may be slow to change (Ployhart and Bliese, 2006). Thus, more time may be needed for students to practice applying AWALP principles to show improvement in these behaviors.

Additional reinforcement of cultural adaptability as a general construct may also be warranted. Although students reported high self-efficacy for, and interest in, cultural adaptability, as well as greater need for cultural adaptability in their current jobs, the absolute level of need for cultural adaptability was lower than what we observed for other adaptive performance dimensions. We conjecture that some students view cultural adaptability as more about national culture than about different social groups more generally; the latter is the focus of AWALP. This supposition is partly supported by a lack of substantial improvement in responses to one of the questions on the knowledge test: On the pretest, 22 percent of the students incorrectly answered a question about cultural adaptability, indicating that it pertains only to a situation involving U.S. Army personnel and Afghans; on the posttest, 18 percent of the students selected this incorrect answer.

Reinforce Knowledge of Adaptive Performance Concepts

One topic for AWG to consider is whether students' scores on the posttraining test are acceptable. As reported in Chapter Three, average scores on the knowledge test were 60 percent correct pretraining and 76 percent correct posttraining. If the posttraining scores are not satisfactory, additional reinforcement of course concepts during classroom instruction and practical exercises may be needed to ensure that students assimilate the material. While the course does not emphasize learning definitions, students need sufficient mastery of course concepts to teach subordinates about adaptive performance and to convince leaders and peers that change is necessary within units. Likewise, if ratings of team performance effectiveness are not satisfactory, additional strategies may be needed to enable students to demonstrate adaptability in team contexts.

Ongoing and Future Evaluation of AWALP

In the following subsections, we recommend ways to strengthen ongoing and future evaluation of AWALP. To provide context for these recommendations, we begin by enumerating both the strengths and limitations of the current study.

Study Strengths and Limitations

The study had a number of strengths:

- We used multiple methods, measures, and types of respondents to provide a comprehensive evaluation.
- Measures targeted multiple levels of adaptive performance, including the individual and the team and the intersection between them.
- We used a pretest–posttest design that controlled for individual characteristics associated with adaptive performance. This allowed us to make inferences with confidence about the effect of AWALP on training outcomes.
- We collected data from students several months after graduation to evaluate application of course principles on the job.
- The evaluation demonstrates methods for measuring intangible training outcomes that did not result in ceiling effects common in studies with similar self-report measures (Baard, Rench, and Kozlowski, 2014). Thus, the approach may be applicable to evaluating a wide range of training efforts that emphasizes 21st-century soldier skills.

However, in addition to these strengths, there are also limitations:

- Participation in AWALP is not random, and there may be selection effects in terms of students who participate (e.g., that they are selected for having strong leadership skills or potential). We attempted to control for these effects by measuring individual characteristics. Nonetheless, generalizability of the results to a broader sample of students needs to be tested.
- Because this was a field study rather than a randomized controlled trial, it is not possible to attribute improvement in outcomes or effects on participants' jobs unequivocally to the course.
- We relied largely on survey methods; therefore, our outcomes may still be subject to biases or other problems that occur with self-report measures, such as social desirability (as suggested by the peer ratings) and careless responding. On the other hand, as noted in Roselle, 2013, and as evident in the prior surveys used to evaluate AWALP discussed in Chapter Two, the changes that we observed in students' ratings (e.g., self-efficacy) may underestimate the effect of the course because students learn that they were not as adaptable as they thought initially.
- Although we used established instruments to measure some constructs, we created original items for others (e.g., declarative knowledge and team performance) with unknown construct validity.
- Finally, while results indicate that some transfer of training is occurring, our results were based primarily on graduates' perceptions of their behavior; we do not have independent assessments of their job performance because of challenges in recruiting graduates' supervisors for follow-up interviews.

We next propose additional approaches to measuring outcomes to address some of the limitations, reduce the response burden, and make the evaluation effort more efficient.

Recommended Measures and Processes for Ongoing Evaluation

The following subsections summarize recommendations for the ongoing evaluation of AWALP and provide some more in-depth discussion on each point. While we recommend continuing use of the current instruments, we propose changes in how they are used.

Continue Use of Current Instruments

We recommend that AWG continue to administer the knowledge test and questions about attitudes toward adaptive performance and leader practice (self-efficacy, interest, and need) at the beginning and end of training and to administer the questions measuring reactions to the course at the end of training. In addition to obtaining feedback about the course, continuing to collect this data can provide the volume of responses needed for more comprehensive assessment of reliability and validity of the measures. We propose a number of changes in use of these measures, as discussed in the next section.

We also recommend continuing to collect information from graduates through telephone interviews to assess how they are using AWALP principles and to identify lessons learned to improve AWALP. We suggest interviewing all graduates in the next two to three AWALP classes, then sampling students from subsequent classes. We discuss collecting data from supervisors in the section on future evaluation of AWALP.

Modify Selected Measures in the Surveys and Team Ratings Instrument

We propose a number of revisions to the survey instruments to further reduce response burden.[2] First, for routinely evaluating AWALP, we recommend eliminating the measures of personality characteristics and dispositional traits from the pretraining survey, although AWG may wish to include demographic characteristics to document and understand the student population(s). However, if AWG seeks to conduct additional research on the criterion-related validity of AWALP training (i.e., the association of training outcomes with subsequent job performance), it would be useful to include measures of cognitive ability and personality and dispositional traits (conscientiousness, extraversion, openness to experience, and learning goal orientation). The

---

[2] As indicated in Chapters Three and Four, we recommend eliminating peer evaluations and "importance" ratings in future evaluations.

International Personality Item Pool, which measures the Big Five personality traits (Goldberg et al., 2006), and the Button, Mathieu and Zajac, 1996, measure of learning goal orientation are available in the public domain.

Second, our team-level measures focused on how adaptive performance dimensions manifested at the group level, but AWALP also focuses on other aspects of team collaboration and performance. In concert with our recommendation to modify the curriculum to address team processes in more depth, we recommend modifying the team rating instrument to include assessment of group-level process, such as planning, mutual monitoring, and backup behavior (Burke, Stagl, et al., 2006, and Smith-Jentsch et al., 1998; see also Shanahan et al., 2007). Such an instrument as the Anti-Air Teamwork Observation Measure (ATOM) could also be used. The ATOM was developed as part of the Tactical Decision Making Under Stress project and measures behaviors reflecting four dimensions of team processes: information exchange, communication, supporting behavior, and leadership and initiative (Smith-Jentsch et al., 1998).

We provided instruments with proposed revisions and the ATOM in a separate report to AWG.

Manage and Streamline Data Collection Procedures

Because the current evaluation was conducted for research, we used some data collection procedures that are not required if AWG evaluates AWALP for quality improvement on an ongoing basis. Simplified procedures can ease response burden and may improve student responsiveness. For example, we protected student confidentiality by not sharing individual results with anyone else outside the research team, including guides. For some measures, such as students' ratings of their teams, responses were submitted anonymously. Students might respond more carefully to the questions if they were aware that guides would review the results (e.g., on the knowledge test) or display them in AARs (e.g., students' ratings of teams); at the same time, the data should be collected in a way that encourages students to be forthright. Therefore, we recommend not sharing individual scores or ratings (e.g., in the case of ratings of teams, guides could average ratings of members within a team). When possible, ratings should be collected anonymously (or by team number rather than student name), but some responses must be identified to calculate pretraining-posttraining differences. This can be done by assigning code numbers to students. Whether code numbers or names are used, we recommend maintaining the confidentiality of students' test scores and survey responses.

We also recommend administering the instruments online rather than using paper-and-pencil instruments. Collecting the data through computers or mobile device can eliminate errors that occur through data entry of paper surveys, and responses can be scored immediately. Computerized entry can also provide information about the quality of students' responses (i.e., "think time"). For example, low scores on the knowledge test or response patterns on surveys (e.g., selecting the same response to each question) coupled with extremely short response times may indicate that students did not take the test or survey seriously. (Long response times, on the other hand, are less meaningful, as one does not know what respondents are doing during the time intervals.)

Recommendations for Future Evaluation of AWALP

Additional methods and measures can contribute to a more comprehensive evaluation of AWALP. Our recommendations are as follows:

- Assess training transfer and results:
  - Develop forms for guides to rate the effectiveness of individual performance in AWALP.
  - Analyze association of effectiveness in AWALP with subsequent adaptive performance effectiveness on the job using supervisor ratings or 360-degree feedback.
  - Compare results for trained and untrained individuals or units.
- Conduct behavioral observations.
- Create additional indicators of AWALP impact:
  - Assess sustainability of graduates' attitudes toward AWALP and toward adaptability.
  - Track other measures of AWALP success, such as repeat business and requests for local instantiations of adaptability training.

The subsections below discuss these recommendations in more detail. Many of these approaches are also relevant to other courses that focus on adaptability. A theme of many of these recommendations is the need to obtain additional measures of adaptable performance.

Assess Training Transfer and Results

The most important topic for future evaluation of AWALP is assessing transfer of training by assessing its criterion-related validity. A study of this nature would assess the association of outcomes measured in training and individual characteristics with subsequent job performance, where graduates' supervisors would provide quantifiable ratings of job performance effectiveness. (This would also require developing a rating form for supervisors to complete.) Comparing performance ratings for graduates with a matched control group of leaders who have not attended AWALP would strengthen this approach. This approach could be extended to studying the effectiveness of teams whose leaders or members have (or have not) participated in AWALP, or to results of entire units that have (or have not) gone through adaptability training.[3]

While studies of criterion-related validity could use students' self-efficacy ratings as a predictor variable, a stronger approach would use expert (i.e., guide) ratings of the effectiveness of individual performance in AWALP (e.g., see section on behavioral observations below). We did not ask the guides to rate individual students because the study already imposed a rather large response burden and because we attempted to obtain ratings of individuals from peers (which was not successful). In addition to providing a source of data to study the criterion-related validity of AWALP, guide ratings of individual effectiveness in AWALP

---

[3]   When undertaking a study of training transfer, we also recommend revisiting the research literature on the association of individual characteristics and adaptability. Baard, Rench, and Kozlowski, 2014, notes the need for stronger theory about individual differences and adaptive performance. Other recent efforts indicate that the relationships may be complex (Dorsey, Cortina, and Luchman, 2010; LePine et al., 2000; Zaccaro, 2007). For example, LePine et al., 2000, suggests that the dependability facet of conscientiousness may be detrimental to making decisions when the rules change, while the achievement facet of conscientiousness may be associated with more-accurate decisions. Zaccaro, 2007, argues that combinations of traits that are integrated in theoretically meaningful ways are more likely to predict leadership than are independent contributions of single traits.

could serve as a source of feedback to students and could be compared with students' knowledge test scores and self-efficacy ratings to assess the construct validity of these measures.

For the criterion measure, i.e., supervisors' ratings of graduates' performance, modifying recruiting processes may improve success in contacting supervisors. Recommendations to recruit supervisors include the following:

- Track who sends students to AWALP to obtain supervisor contact information on enrollment.[4]
- Contact immediate supervisors (for platoon sergeant, contact the platoon leader; for section leader, contact the platoon sergeant, etc.).
- Given frequent personnel changes, contact supervisors after three months rather than later.
- Give priority for future AWALP enrollments to supervisors who provide feedback about course graduates.

Assessing transfer of training could be expanded further by collecting 360-degree feedback for graduates and a matched sample of leaders who have not attended AWALP. Using 360-degree feedback, rather than relying on supervisory ratings alone, might reduce common rater errors, such as halo error (see Baard, Rench, and Kozlowski, 2014). The Army already has a 360-degree evaluation process in place for officers in the Multi-Source Assessment and Feedback Program (U.S. Army, undated), which could serve as a starting point for this effort. Many of the items on the evaluation form are directly relevant to adaptability; examples include "Adapts quickly to new situations and requirements"; "Improves ability in interpersonal interaction"; "Maintains relevant cultural understanding"; "Is open to diverse ideas and points of view"; and "Coaches others in the development or improvement of skills." However, because some of the items on the form are at odds with adaptability principles, the form would need some revision. For

---

[4] Tracking enrollment in this way would also facilitate tracking repeat business (i.e., multiple enrollments on the part of individual supervisors) to use as an additional indicator of AWALP success.

example, "Prioritizes tasks for teams or groups" and "Makes appropriate assignments or role delegation to subordinates or teams" convey a top-down rather than a bottom-up approach. A related effort could examine the attitudes and knowledge of graduates' (and a matched sample's) subordinates to assess whether graduates have successfully disseminated AWALP principles to the soldiers that they lead.

As described by Salas et al., 2012, a wide range of other factors influence training transfer. These can include characteristics of trainees (additional to those examined in this study), how training is designed and executed, and features of the work environment. A comprehensive analysis will examine these factors to understand and improve training transfer.

Conduct Behavioral Observations

We recommend conducting systematic behavioral observations during the course to evaluate individual and team performance and to assess performance improvement as the course progresses (for a review of behavioral measures, see Wildman et al., 2011). We propose that AWG use event-based measures or behavior checklists, in which trained observers (i.e., guides) record critical behaviors as determined by subject-matter experts. In AWALP, critical behaviors would be linked to the dimensions of adaptive performance (e.g., see White et al., 2005) and other team behaviors relevant to each exercise. Event-based measures have been used in prior studies of team adaptation and performance; some approaches involve documenting the frequency of specific behaviors, while others include more detailed assessments of the quality of those behaviors (e.g., see Entin et al., 1993; Smith-Jentsch et al., 1998). In a study of AWALP, Roselle, 2013, used behavior checklists and found increased frequencies of adaptive behaviors in similar practical exercises conducted at the beginning and end of the course.

A primary advantage of checklists is that they are less susceptible to some of the biases common in self-report measures or in subjective ratings of the frequency or quality of behaviors. However, checklists have some drawbacks. They are more labor intensive to use than subjective ratings, and an effort must be made to establish interrater reliability among observers. Ratings may also be influenced by observers' expectations about performance improvement as the course progresses. In the case of assessing improvement by using parallel practical exercises, additional challenges include establishing the equivalence of the exercises and requiring added time in the curriculum. Some of these issues could be addressed by having subject-matter experts who are naïve to the course structure rate video clips of students engaged in course activities. This approach would eliminate the need for equivalent exercises and would reduce or eliminate biases associated with expectations for performance that might occur if these observations were conducted by individuals with in-depth knowledge of the curriculum. However, because these ratings would be conducted post hoc, they would be more useful for research than for providing feedback to students during the course.

Create Additional Indicators of AWALP Impact

In addition to measures of individual effectiveness training and subsequent performance on the job, AWG may wish to assess the sustainability of graduates' attitudes toward AWALP and toward adaptive performance principles using follow-up online surveys beyond the three- or six-month points after graduation. As another measure of success, AWG can track repeat business (i.e., multiple enrollments on the part of the same units). In addition, a number of different divisions have asked AWG for support in standing up local adaptability training modeled after AWALP. These requests can serve as other indicators of AWALP success.

Expanding AWALP's Approach to Adaptability Training

Below we discuss two possible ways that AWALP's approach to adaptability training might be expanded. One option is to increase the number of students receiving training, either by increasing throughput or by infusing the AWALP approach into other professional military education (PME) courses. Another option is to create a follow-on course that expands adaptability instruction at the team level.

Increase the Number of Students Receiving Training

The Army should consider ways to leverage AWG's approach and disseminate AWALP principles more broadly. We propose two options for expanding AWALP. One is to increase the number of trainees in the existing course or modified versions of it. AWG could continue to stand up local versions of AWALP in divisions by training local trainers or through mobile training teams.

Another way to disseminate AWALP more broadly is to incorporate adaptability principles into existing PME courses. Army courses for NCOs that currently develop adaptability skills include the advanced leader and the senior leader courses. For officers, relevant Army courses would include the Basic Officer Leader Course, the Captains' Career Course, and intermediate-level education. To modify a course, the Army would first have to determine specifically how AWALP training differs from the course's current approach to training adaptability skills and then determine the actions needed and the resources required to make the appropriate changes. For example, successfully transforming existing courses would require additional training development resources to modify the POI and course materials, along with instructor training to implement the new approach. It might also require different facilities, equipment, personnel, or other training resources at training bases. In addition, evaluations would be needed to assess the degree of improvement in training outcomes and determine whether the improvements are worth the costs of the change.

To support expansion of AWG's approach to adaptability training, we recommend that AWG create a training support package with a POI and supplementary materials to support diffusion of adaptability training to the Army at large. While a conventional Army POI (e.g., specifying tasks, conditions, and standards) may not be appropriate for AWALP in light of its teaching approach, a set of organized materials will help preserve institutional knowledge related to training adaptability and will support dissemination of course content and instructional methods. It would also enable assessment of how well guides in other implementations of adaptability training adhere to the principles of the original implementation. Research in other domains (e.g., evidence-based practice of medicine; Watkins et al., 2011) suggests that, even with clear and strict guidelines, there may be deviations from protocol; given the teaching approach applied in AWALP, it may be even more important to exercise care and attention to appropriate implementation.

Create a Follow-On Course That Expands Instruction at the Team Level

TRADOC can support mission command principles further by expanding on instruction of team adaptive performance, as described earlier. AWALP provides a starting point for training soldiers to work in and lead teams, but there are many additional topics to address to foster effective teams and effective team leaders. Some of these topics (e.g., shared mental models) could be addressed in more depth in AWALP, but given the large and growing literature relevant to team adaptation, we recommend developing a follow-on course focused exclusively on these topics. In addition, some existing leader development institutional courses or other training that focuses on making teams more effective might provide an appropriate context for this training. Examples of prospective team-based topics to expand upon or to address in training include the following:

- **Shared mental models.** The concept of team or shared mental models is discussed in AWALP and could be explored in more depth in other courses so that soldiers understand how shared mental models influence team adaptation, how to foster shared mental models, and the conditions in which team mental models are beneficial or detrimental to performance. Mental models are frameworks of knowledge and processes that represent and guide our interpretation of data in the world. Team mental models, which are distinct from the sum of team members' individual cognitions (Klimoski and Mohammed, 1994), influence the process and content of decisionmaking (Walsh and Fahey, 1986). Shared mental models are important for team training, performance, and adaptability, can reduce intrateam conflict, and influence adaptive decisionmaking in a variety of domains (Cannon-Bowers, Salas, and Converse, 1993; Fiore, Ross, and Jentsch, 2012; Lim and Klein, 2006; Marks, Zaccaro, and Mathieu, 2000; Randall,

Resick, and DeChurch, 2011). Interestingly, research has demonstrated that similar mental models are more beneficial in novel situations than in common or routine situations (Marks, Zaccaro, and Mathieu, 2000). Unfortunately, persistent mental models can also be detrimental to adaptability. Case studies of disasters have shown a recurring theme of poorly constructed and obstinate mental models in the face of changing situations (Smith and Dowell, 2000; Weick, 1990; Weick, 1993). In particular, dynamic conditions require teams to reinvent their models (Uitdewilligen, Waller, and Zijlstra, 2010).

- **Transactive memory systems.** These are related to shared mental models but are specific to members' knowledge about "who knows what" in the team. Transactive memory systems have been observed to be a significant predictor of team performance, group learning, and creativity (e.g., Austin, 2003; Gino et al., 2010; Liang, Moreland, and Argote, 1995) and are particularly beneficial when engaging in nonroutine work or in turbulent conditions (Akgün et al., 2005; Ren, Carley, and Argote, 2006). Students in a team-training course can learn how to foster development of these systems, e.g., by composing stable teams (Akgün et al., 2005; Littlepage, Robison, and Reddington, 1997), composing smaller versus larger groups (e.g., Jackson and Moreland, 2009), training team members on their tasks together versus individually (Liang, Moreland, and Argote, 1995), and investing in the planning stages to determine who has what expertise (Rulke and Rau, 2000).
- **Team trust.** Mutual trust is an underlying principle of developing cohesive teams, which in turn, is a central element of mission command doctrine (ADP 6-0, 2012). Trust is related to the concept of psychological safety discussed earlier (Burke, Stagl, et al., 2006). A team training course can address how trust develops in teams and how to foster mutual trust and cohesion.
- **Process losses.** When working on cognitive tasks, such as generating ideas, making judgments, and solving problems, teams are subject to a variety of process losses (Steiner, 1972) or factors that prevent teams from being as effective they can be. Examples

of common process losses include suppression of ideas, failure to share information that is critical to the task, polarized decisions, and pressures toward uniformity. Numerous studies have diagnosed the causes of such losses and have identified strategies to avoid these pitfalls of team interaction (e.g., for a brief review, see Straus, Parker, and Bruce, 2011).

- **Team facilitation.** Team facilitation can foster performance; for example, in brainstorming, skilled facilitators can help teams avoid process losses by keeping the group focused on the task, by encouraging contributions without criticism (thereby reducing evaluation apprehension), and by soliciting contributions from quieter group members (thereby reducing social loafing) (Offner, Kramer, and Winter, 1996; Paulus et al., 2006). Facilitators can learn to use a variety of other strategies that pertain to group composition, structure, and process to enable teams to capitalize on members' knowledge and skills (see Straus, Parker, and Bruce, 2011). While AWALP provides some opportunities for students to serve in team leadership roles, additional practical experience in using strategies for facilitation could be beneficial.

Other topics in research on teams that are relevant to adaptability include goal setting, conflict resolution, and working in distributed groups.

Lessons for Adaptability Evaluation in Other Training Contexts

This research can provide lessons about measuring adaptability and other intangible concepts not only in AWALP but in other training contexts. In addition to using the methods and measures developed for this study to assess local versions of AWALP, the research could be applied to designing evaluations of PME courses that address adaptive performance. This will become particularly important as the Army seeks to push adaptability training into the mainstream institutional training domain.

The evaluation demonstrates the benefits of using multiple measures and methods and documents how such measures can be developed and implemented. Evaluation of other courses that involve adaptability training can make use of most of the reaction measures implemented in this study "as is" or with minor modifications. Pre-post knowledge tests, attitudinal measures (e.g., self-efficacy), and post-graduate interviews can be used with appropriate revisions for course content. Instructor and student ratings of team performance may be broadly applicable to Army training. Continued use of these instruments, including the modifications and more comprehensive efforts as suggested above, can provide data to validate the measures, supporting TRADOC and contributing to the research literature. More fundamentally, robust studies of transfer performance could provide evidence that adaptability is indeed an aspect of performance that can be improved through training. This would rebut alternative views, such as Individual ADAPTability theory (e.g., Ployhart and Bliese, 2006), which conceives of adaptability primarily as a set of individual differences that are relatively stable and thus better attained in an organization by recruiting the right kind of individual rather than by training.

In addition, it has been over a decade since Pulakos and colleagues developed their model (Pulakos et al., 2000), and the body of theory and empirical research on adaptability has since been growing, particularly at individual and team levels. For example, adaptation is defined in AWALP as a performance construct, which Baard, Rench, and Kozlowski, 2014, classified as an individual difference. Alternative theoretical approaches consider adaptation as performance change or as a process, which are more conducive to training (rather than selection) strategies (Baard, Rench, and Kozlowski, 2014). The course material in AWALP already emphasizes many of the processes by which individuals and teams can be adaptive that are explicated in these alternative perspectives, and use of one of these theoretical models may be helpful as an organizing framework for the course. AWG should also continue to stay apprised of the growing literature to ensure that the key concepts addressed in the curriculum are consistent with research on adaptation.

Conclusion

The shift in Army doctrine from command and control to mission command calls for profound changes in leader and team conduct. General Dempsey has noted that mission command principles—which emphasize a bottom-up rather than a top-down approach—must become institutional in Army doctrine and in Army training (Dempsey, 2011). Thus, this change in philosophy requires a concomitant transformation in training. AWG's successful development and implementation of AWALP exemplifies mission command principles in terms of both the content of the course and how it is taught. AWALP, supported by systematic course evaluation, provides a promising approach for the Army as it seeks to further develop adaptable leaders and teams.

Typical AWALP-Like Practical Exercise: One Rope Bridge

To preserve the integrity of the course, the following example does not come from the AWALP curriculum, but it is typical of AWALP practical exercises.

Purpose
"One Rope Bridge" is an exercise that illustrates many of the teaching concepts and the instructional approach used in AWALP.
In this exercise, each member of a four- to five-person team is taught a different knot; collectively, these enable the group to construct a one-rope bridge. The team must figure out where and how each knot should be located to construct the bridge.

Dimensions of Adaptive Performance and Other Skills Taught	
• Learning new tasks and procedures • Dealing with ambiguous situations • Problem solving	• Critical thinking • Accountability • Teamwork

Actions
Students watch a short video about a vehicle losing its load on a public roadway. The guide leads a brief discussion about the video and presents objectives and expectations for the activity.
The "pretest" phase of the exercise is used to determine whether any participants are familiar with the knots being taught; these students then help coach their teammates. Alternatively, the first team member who masters the knots then assists the others.
In phase 1, team members work independently to learn specific knots. Peer training is followed by practice and a check on learning. There is no reference to a rope bridge in this phase.
Students are given a break prior to phase 2. This can be a lunch break or a delay as long as 1–2 days.
In phase 2, teams are presented with a practical problem that requires all members of the team and their equipment to cross an obstacle in 20 minutes. Essentially, the task requires the team to construct a one-rope bridge. Collectively the group will know how to tie the component parts of the bridge; however, they must solve the problems of where and how to place each knot to construct the bridge.

AAR Questions	
Phase 1	**Phase 2**
• How did we go about helping you develop a new skill? • How difficult was this for you? • Were you focused on passing the test or getting better? • Did time cause you any concerns? • How does this model compare to how the Army traditionally teaches a class?	• What was key to the group's success? • Did you accomplish the mission? • If not, what was the reason(s)? • Did you complete the mission? • What was the learning environment like (both phases)? • How was the learning activity structured? • Characterize the instruction • What 21st-century skills were exercised here?

Items Assessing Reactions to Training

Below are the questions used to assess reactions to training. Items with the same letter in parentheses were combined into scales as described in Chapter Three.

Table B.1
Questions Assessing Reactions to Training

Question	Response Options
1. AWALP guides were knowledgeable about the subject matter (a)	Strongly disagree to strongly agree
2. AWALP guides effectively facilitated AARs and group discussions (a)	
3. AWALP guides effectively facilitated course exercises (a)	
4. AWALP guides provided sufficient feedback on my individual performance	
5. AWALP guides provided sufficient feedback on team performance	
6. The feedback I received from AWALP guides enhanced my learning[a]	
7. Team members provided relevant feedback on my performance	
8. Course materials supported the learning objectives	
9. AWALP training facilities were satisfactory	

Table B.1—Continued

Question	Response Options
10. Please indicate the degree to which you agree or disagree that your abilities in the following areas have improved as a result of participating in AWALP:	
a. Performing in uncertain situations (b)	
b. Training others (b)	
c. Conducting AARs (b)	
d. Interacting with people from different cultures (b)	
e. Thinking creatively (b)	
f. Being self aware (b)	
g. Solving problems (b)	
h. Handling emergencies (b)	
i. Performing under stress (b)	
j. Coaching others (b)	
k. Being confident on the job (b)	
11. Pick the two topics from Question 10a – k above that you think have changed most as a result of AWALP. How will your performance in these two areas be different in the future?	Open-ended
12. Pick the two topics from Question 10a – k above that you think have changed least during AWALP. Why will your performance in these two areas not be different?	
13. Overall, I was satisfied with what I learned from AWALP (c)	Strongly disagree to strongly agree
14. Attending AWALP was a good use of my time (c)	
15. AWALP is relevant to my career (c)	
16. I would recommend AWALP to others (c)	
a. Why or why not?	Open-ended
17. The length of the course was	Too short, about right, too long
18. The amount of time spent in the classroom (compared to hands-on activities) was	Too little, about right, too much
19. The classroom portions of the course were	Too academic, about right, mostly common sense

Table B.1—Continued

Question	Response Options
20. The exercises in the course were	Too difficult, about right, too easy
21. What aspects of AWALP should be changed? How would you change them?	Open-ended
22. Are there any other ways that AWALP will change the way you lead others that you haven't described in your other answers? If so, how?	
23. Do you anticipate challenges applying what you have learned in AWALP? If so, what are they?	

[a] The mean rating for this item was the same as the mean for Item 5 and was not shown in Figure 3.1.

Main Effects and Interactions of Individual Characteristics and Attitudes Toward Adaptive Performance

Table C.1 indicates statistically significant main effects of individual characteristics on self-efficacy for and interest in adaptive performance dimensions and leader practice. In most of these cases, individual characteristics were associated with pretraining but not posttraining outcome measures.

Table C.2 shows significant interactions of individual characteristics and time, which occurred for a small number of outcomes:

- The change in self-efficacy for creative thinking depended on openness to experience, such that the change was larger for students who reported lower openness to experience. The course thus had a greater impact on self-efficacy for creative thinking for students with lower levels of openness to experience, and the course had less (or no) impact on self-efficacy for creative thinking for students with higher levels of openness to experience, holding the other individual characteristics constant. The change in interest in creative thinking depended on motivation for training, such that students who anticipated that they would benefit more from the course showed a greater increase in interest for creative thinking compared with students who expected fewer benefits from the course.

- The change in self-efficacy for interpersonal adaptability and decisionmaking under stress depended on time in service. The course

Table C.1
Main Effects of Individual Characteristics on Self-Efficacy (E) and Interest (I)

Effect or Characteristic	Dimension						
	Creative Thinking	Ambiguous Situations	Learning	Interpersonal	Cultural	Decisionmaking Under Stress	Leader Practice
Pre-post change	E,I	E,I	E,I	E,I	E,I	E,I	E,I
Openness	E,I						
Extraversion	E	E,I	E	E	E	I	E
Conscientiousness					I		
Mastery orientation	E,I	E,I	E,I	I	E,I	I	I
Performance orientation						I[a]	
Time in service	E		E	E	E		E
Motivation for training							E

[a] This relationship was negative, i.e., students with a higher performance orientation were less interested in being in situations requiring decisionmaking under stress.

Table C.2
Interactions of Time (Pre-Post Scores) with Individual Characteristics for Self-Efficacy (E) and Interest (I)

Characteristic	Dimension						
	Creative Thinking	Ambiguous Situations	Learning	Interpersonal	Cultural	Decisionmaking Under Stress	Leader Practice
Openness	E						
Extraversion					E		
Conscientiousness					I		
Mastery orientation					E,I		
Performance orientation							
Time in service				E		E	
Motivation for training	I						

had a greater impact on these dimensions for students with less time in service, and the course had minimal or no impact on these dimensions for students with greater time in service, holding the other individual characteristics constant.

• The change in self-efficacy and interest for cultural adaptability depended on a mastery learning goal orientation. The course had a greater impact on self-efficacy and interest for cultural adaptability for students with lower mastery orientation, and the course had minimal or no impact on self-efficacy and interest for cultural adaptability for students with higher mastery orientation, holding the other individual characteristics constant. The change in interest in cultural adaptability also depended on conscientiousness, showing a similar pattern of results (i.e., greater change in interest in cultural adaptability for students with lower conscientiousness).

Interview Questions

Questions for Graduates

1. Are there ways in which you feel you have changed professionally as a result of the AWALP training?
2. (If respondent does not address these topics in his or her response): Have you changed how you do the following? Frequency that you do the following?
   a. Coach or mentor subordinates?
   b. Train others in technical skills/procedures?
   c. Train others for physical strength/endurance?
   d. Train others to work effectively in teams?
   e. Train others to solve complex problems?
   f. Conduct an AAR?
   g. Brief a commanding officer?
   h. Delegate responsibilities to others?
   i. Seek and use input from subordinates about a complex decision?
3. (For behaviors listed above that did not change), why not? Possible prompts:
   a. Opportunity
   b. Command climate
   c. Necessity on the job
   d. Value of AWALP approach over my previous method

4. (Prompts if interviewee answers "yes" to 2a, 2b, 2c, 2f, 2g, 2h and not already addressed in their answer)
    a. What are the key skills and/or personal characteristics necessary to effectively (2a, 2b, 2c, 2f, 2g, 2h)?
    b. In what ways does your (2a, 2b, 2c, 2f, 2g, 2h) differ from before AWALP?
    c. Were others receptive or unreceptive to your changes to (2a, 2b, 2c, 2f, 2g, 2h)?
        i.   If unreceptive, how did you handle that?
        ii. If receptive, how did they respond?
5. (Prompts if interviewee answers "yes" to 2d, 2e, 2i)
    a. Describe an example
        ii.   What was the situation?
        iii. What did you do?
        iv.   What was the result?
6. (If the answers to 2a–2i were "yes"): We are interested in how your experience at AWALP affects soldiers in your unit/organization.
    a. Who in your organization has been affected because of your changes?
    b. Who is most affected by those changes?
    c. Do you think your commander is aware of the changes?
    d. Who is the best person/people at the unit level to comment on how AWALP has affected former students?
7. Looking back on your experience in AWALP, are there any changes that you would recommend making to the course?
8. Would you recommend AWALP to others?
    a. If so, what type of person could benefit the most by the experience?
    b. If not, why not?
9. Do you have any other feedback about the AWALP training that you did not share through the end-of-course survey or through this interview?

Questions for Graduates' Supervisors

1. Did you have a role in determining who went to AWALP?
   a. If yes, what were the reasons for selecting whom you selected? Would you use different reasons for future selections?
2. Have you noticed ways that the AWALP graduates changed following their return?
   a. If so, how? Possible prompts:
      ii. Interact with subordinates (delegate, train, coach)
      iii. Conduct AARs
      iv. Communicate with you
3. Do you have any other comments about AWALP training?

APPENDIX E

Change in Students' Pre-Post Responses Regarding Need for Adaptive Performance

These figures show the degree of change in students' pre-post response to questions about the need for adaptive performance in their current jobs. The response options were "never," "a few times/year," "monthly," "weekly," and "daily."

For example, for cultural adaptability shown in Figure E.1, 20 percent of the students changed their responses by two or more categories, indicating a greater need for being adaptive (e.g., from "never" to "monthly" or from "monthly" to "daily"). Thirty-two percent of the students changed their responses by one category (e.g., from "monthly" to "weekly" or from "weekly" to "daily"). Thirty-seven percent did not change their answers. Some students also reported less need for being adaptive; 8 percent dropped by one category and 3 percent dropped by two or more categories.

Figure E.1
Degree of Pretraining-Postraining Change in Responses Regarding Need
for Adaptive Performance Dimensions in Current Job

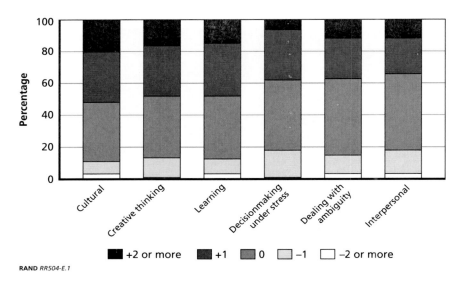

Figure E.2
Degree of Pretraining-Postraining Change in Responses Regarding Need for Leader Behaviors in Current Job

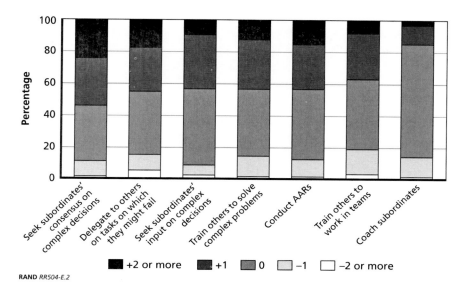

RAND *RR504-E.2*

References

38th Army Chief of Staff, "CSA Strategic Priorities," October 2013. As of December 20, 2013:
http://usarmy.vo.llnwd.net/e2/c/downloads/316390.pdf

ADP—*See* Army Doctrine Publication.

Akgün, Ali E., John Byrne, Halit Keskin, Gary S. Lynn, and Salih Z. Imamoglu, "Knowledge Networks in New Product Development Projects: A Transactive Memory Perspective," *Information & Management*, Vol. 42, 2005, pp. 1105–1120.

Alvarez, Kaye, Eduardo Salas, and Christina M. Garofano, "An Integrated Model of Training Evaluation and Effectiveness," *Human Resource Development Review*, Vol. 3, No. 4, 2004, pp. 385–416.

Anderson, John R., Lynne Reder, and Herbert A. Simon, "Situated Learning and Education," *Educational Researcher*, Vol. 25, No. 4, 1996, pp. 5–11.

Army Doctrine Publication 6-0, *Mission Command*, Washington, D.C.: Headquarters Department of Army, 2012.

Army Field Manual 6-22, *Army Leadership: Competent, Confident, and Agile*, Washington, D.C.: Headquarters, Department of the Army, October 2006.

Asymmetric Warfare Adaptive Leader Program, *Leader's Guide for Enhancing Adaptability*, December 2011.

Austin, John R., "Transactive Memory in Organizational Groups: The Effects of Content, Consensus, Specialization, and Accuracy on Group Performance," *Journal of Applied Psychology*, Vol. 88, 2003, pp. 866–878.

Baard, Samantha K., Tara A. Rench, and Steve W. Kozlowski, "Performance Adaptation: A Theoretical Integration and Review," *Journal of Management*, Vol. 40, No. 1, 2014, pp. 1–52.

Barrick, Murray R., and Michael K. Mount, "The Big Five Personality Dimensions and Job Performance: A Meta-Analysis," *Personnel Psychology*, Vol. 44, 1991, pp. 1–26.

Bartone, Paul T., Scott A. Snook, and Trueman R. Tremble, Jr., "Cognitive and Personality Predictors of Leader Performance in West Point Cadets," *Military Psychology*, Vol. 14, No. 4, 2002, pp. 321–338.

Burke, C. Shawn, Linda G. Pierce, and Eduardo Salas, eds., *Understanding Adaptability: A Prerequisite for Effective Performance Within Complex Environments*, Emerald Group Publishing Limited, 2006.

Burke, C. Shawn, Kevin C. Stagl, Eduardo Salas, Linda Pierce, and Dane Kendall, "Understanding Team Adaptation: A Conceptual Analysis and Model," *Journal of Applied Psychology*, Vol. 91, No. 6, 2006, pp. 1189–1207.

Button, Scott B., John E. Mathieu, and Dennis M. Zajac, "The Development and Psychometric Evaluation of Measures of Learning Goal and Performance Goal Orientation," *Organizational Behavior and Human Decision Processes*, Vol. 67, 1996, pp. 26–48.

Campbell, John P., "Modeling the Performance Prediction Problem in Industrial and Organizational Psychology," in M. D. Dunnette and L. M. Hough, eds., *Handbook of Industrial and Organizational Psychology*, Palo Alto, Calif.: Consulting Psychologists Press, Inc., 1990, pp. 687–732.

Campbell, John P., Rondey A. McCloy, Scott H. Oppler, and Christopher E. Sager, "A Theory of Performance," in N. Schmitt and W. C. Borman, eds., *Personnel Selection in Organizations*, San Francisco: Jossey-Bass, 1993, pp. 35–70.

Cannon-Bowers, Janis A., Eduardo Salas, and Sharolyn Converse, "Shared Mental Models in Expert Team Decision Making," in N. J. Castellan, Jr., ed., *Individual and Group Decision Making*, Hillsdale, N.J.: Lawrence Erlbaum Associates, 1993, pp. 221–246.

Chen, Gilad, Brian Thomas, and J. Craig Wallace, "A Multilevel Examination of the Relationships Among Training Outcomes, Mediating Regulatory Processes, and Adaptive Performance," *Journal of Applied Psychology*, Vol. 90, 2005, pp. 827–841.

Cohen, Jacob, *Statistical Power Analysis for the Behavioral Sciences*, Hillsdale, N.J.: Lawrence Erlbaum Assoc., 1988.

Costa, Paul T., and Robert R. McCrae, "NEO™ Personality Inventory-3 (NEO™-PI-3)," Odessa, Fla.: Psychological Assessment Resources, Inc., 2010.

Dempsey, Martin E., *The US Army Learning Concept for 2015*, Fort Monroe, Va.: Department of the Army, Headquarters U.S. TRADOC, PAM 525-8-2, 2011. As of September 17, 2014:
http://www.tradoc.army.mil/tpubs/pams/tp525-8-2.pdf

Dorsey, David W., Jose M. Cortina, and Joseph Luchman, "Adaptive and Citizenship-Related Behaviors at Work," in J. L. Tippins and N. T. Farr, eds., *Handbook of Employee Selection*, New York: Routledge, 2010, pp. 463–487.

Dweck, Carol S., "Motivational Processes Affecting Learning," *American Psychologist*, Vol. 86, No. 10, 1986, pp. 1040–1048.

Entin, Eileen B., Elliot E. Entin, Jean MacMillan, and Daniel Serfaty, *Structuring and Training High-Reliability Teams Year 1 Report*, U.S. ALPHATECH Inc., November 1993.

Entin, Elliot E., and Daniel Serfaty, "Adaptive Team Coordination," *Human Factors: The Journal of the Human Factors and Ergonomics Society*, Vol. 41, No. 2, 1999, pp. 312–325.

Fiore, Stephen M., Karol G. Ross, and Florian Jentsch, "A Team Cognitive Readiness Framework for Small-Unit Training," *Journal of Cognitive Engineering and Decision Making*, Vol. 6, No. 3, 2012, pp. 325–349.

Fisher, Sandra L., and J. Kevin Ford, "Differential Effects of Learner Effort and Goal Orientation on Two Learning Outcomes," *Personnel Psychology*, Vol. 51, 1998, pp. 397-420.

Gagne, Robert M., Walter W. Wager, Katherine Golas, and John M. Keller, *Principles of Instructional Design*, 5th ed., Belmont, Calif.: Wadsworth, Inc., 2005.

Gino, F., L. Argote, E. Miron-Spektor, and G. Todorova, "First, Get Your Feet Wet: The Effects of Learning from Direct and Indirect Experience on Team Creativity," *Organizational Behavior and Human Decision Processes*, Vol. 111, 2010, pp. 102–115.

Goldberg, Lewis R., John A. Johnson, Herbert W. Eber, Robert Hogan, Michael C. Ashton, C. Robert Cloninger, and Harrison C. Gough, "The International Personality Item Pool and the Future of Public-Domain Personality Measures," *Journal of Research in Personality*, Vol. 40, 2006, pp. 84–96.

Griffin, Barbara, and Beryl Hesketh, "Adaptable Behaviours for Successful Work and Career Adjustment," *Australian Journal of Psychology*, Vol. 55, No. 2, 2003, pp. 65–73.

Grossman, Rebecca, and Eduardo Salas, "The Transfer of Training: What Really Matters," *International Journal of Training and Development*, Vol. 15, No. 2, 2011, pp. 103–120.

Hallmark, Bryan W., and S. Jamie Gayton, *Improving Soldier and Unit Effectiveness with the Stryker Brigade Combat Team Warfighters' Forum*, Santa Monica, Calif.: RAND Corporation, TR-919-A, 2011. As of June 24, 2014: http://www.rand.org/pubs/technical_reports/TR919

Haskins, Casey, "A Commander's View of Outcomes-Based Training and Education," in Gary Riccio, Fred Diedrich, and Michael Cortes, eds., *An Initiative in Outcomes-Based Training and Education: Implications for an Integrated Approach to Values-Based Requirements*, Ft. Meade, Md.: Asymmetric Warfare Group, 2010, pp. 342–346.

Hunter, John E., and Ronda F. Hunter, "Validity and Utility of Alternative Predictors of Job Performance," *Psychological Bulletin*, Vol. 96, No. 1, 1984, pp. 72–98.

Jackson, Marina, and Richard L. Moreland, "Transactive Memory in the Classroom," *Small Group Research*, Vol. 40, No. 5, 2009, pp. 508–534.

Judge, Timothy A., and Joyce E. Bono, "Five-Factor Model of Personality and Transformational Leadership," *Journal of Applied Psychology*, Vol. 85, No. 5, 2000, pp. 751–765.

Judge, Timothy A., Joyce E. Bono, Remus Ilies, and Megan W. Gerhardt, "Personality and Leadership: A Qualitative and Quantitative Review," *Journal of Applied Psychology*, Vol. 87, No. 4, 2002, pp. 765–780.

Kirkpatrick, Donald L., *Evaluating Training Programs: The Four Levels*, San Francisco, Calif.: Berrett-Koehler, 1994.

Klein, Howard J., Raymond A. Noe, and Chongwei Wang, "Motivation to Learn and Course Outcomes: The Impact of Delivery Mode, Learning Goal Orientation, and Perceived Barriers and Enablers," *Personnel Psychology*, Vol. 59, 2006, pp. 665–702.

Klimoski, Richard, and Susan Mohammed, "Team Mental Model: Construct or Metaphor?" *Journal of Management*, Vol. 20, No. 2, 1994, pp. 403–437.

Kozlowski, Steve W. J., Stanley M. Gully, Earl R. Nason, and Eleanor M. Smith, "Developing Adaptive Teams: A Theory of Compilation and Performance Across Levels and Time," in Daniel R. Ilgen and Elaine D. Pulakos, eds., *The Changing Nature of Work Performance: Implications for Staffing, Personnel Actions, and Development*, San Francisco: Jossey-Bass, 1999, pp. 240–292.

Kozlowski, Steve W. J., Daniel J. Watola, Jaclyn M. Nowakowski, Brian H. Kim, and Isabel C. Botero, "Developing Adaptive Teams: A Theory of Dynamic Team Leadership," in Eduardo Salas, Gerald F. Goodwin, and C. Shawna Burke, eds., *Team Effectiveness in Complex Organizations: Cross-Disciplinary Perspectives and Approaches*, Mahwah, N.J.: Lawrence Erlbaum, 2009, pp. 113–155.

Lave, Jean, and Etienne Wenger, *Situated Learning: Legitimate Peripheral Participation*, Cambridge, UK: Cambridge University Press, 1991.

LePine, Jeffrey A., Jason A. Colquitt, and Amir Erez, "Adaptability to Changing Task Contexts: Effects of General Cognitive Ability, Conscientiousness, and Openness to Experience," *Personnel Psychology*, Vol. 53, 2000, pp. 563–593.

Liang, Diane Wei, Richard Moreland, and Linda Argote, "Group Versus Individual Training and Group Performance: The Mediating Role of Transactive Memory," *Personality and Social Psychology Bulletin*, Vol. 21, No. 4, 1995, pp. 384–393.

Lim, Beng-Chong, and Katherine J. Klein, "Team Mental Models and Team Performance: A Field Study of the Effects of Team Mental Model Similarity and Accuracy," *Journal of Organizational Behavior*, Vol. 27, 2006, pp. 403–418.

Littlepage, Glenn E., William Robison, and Kelly Reddington, "Effects of Task Experience and Group Experience on Group Performance, Member Ability and Recognition of Expertise," *Organizational Behavior and Human Decision Processes*, Vol. 69, 1997, pp. 133–147.

Marks, Michelle A., Stephen J. Zaccaro, and John E. Mathieu, "Performance Implications of Leader Briefings and Team-Interaction Training for Team Adaptation to Novel Environments," *Journal of Applied Psychology*, Vol. 85, 2000, pp. 971–986.

McGrath, Joseph E., *Groups: Interaction and Performance*, Vol. 14, Englewood Cliffs, N.J.: Prentice-Hall Inc., 1984.

Mesmer-Magnus, Jessica, and Chockalingam Viswesvaran, "Inducing Maximal Versus Typical Learning Through the Provision of a Pretraining Goal Orientation," *Human Performance*, Vol. 20, No. 3, 2007, pp. 205–222.

Morgan, Ben B., Jr., Albert S. Glickman, Elizabeth A. Woodard, Arthur S. Blaiwes, and Eduardo Salas, *Measurement of Team Behaviors in a Navy Environment*, Orlando, Fla: Naval Training Systems Center, Human Factors Division, NTSC TR-86-014, 1986.

Offner, Anne K., Thomas J. Kramer, and Joel P. Winter, "The Effects of Facilitation, Recording, and Pauses on Group Brainstorming," *Small Group Research*, Vol. 27, 1996, pp. 283–298.

Orasanu, Judith, "Shared Problem Models and Flight Crew Performance," in Johnston, N., M. McDonald, and R. Fuller, eds., *Aviation Psychology in Practice*, Aldershot, UK: Ashgate Publishing Group, 1990.

Paulus, Paul B., Toshihiko Nakui, Vicky L. Putman, and Vincent R. Brown, "Effects of Task Instructions and Brief Breaks on Brainstorming," *Group Dynamics: Theory, Research, and Practice*, Vol. 10, No. 3, 2006, pp. 206–219.

Paulus, Paul B., and Huei-Chuan Yang, "Idea Generation in Groups: A Basis for Creativity in Organizations," *Organizational Behavior and Human Decision Processes*, Vol. 82, No. 1, 2000, pp. 76–87.

Phillips, Jean M., and Stanley M. Gully, "Role of Goal Orientation, Ability, Need for Achievement, and Locus of Control in the Self-Efficacy and Goal-Setting Process," *Journal of Applied Psychology*, Vol. 82, No. 5, 1997, pp. 792–802.

Ployhart, Robert E., and Paul D. Bliese, "Individual Adaptability (I-ADAPT) Theory: Conceptualizing the Antecedents, Consequences, and Measurement of Individual Differences in Adaptability," in C. Shawn Burke, Linda G. Pierce, and Eduardo Salas, eds., *Understanding Adaptability: A Prerequisite for Effective Performance Within Complex Environments*, Emerald Group Publishing Limited, 2006, pp. 3–39.

Pulakos, Elaine D., Sharon Arad, Michelle A. Donovan, and Kevin E. Plamondon, "Adaptability in the Workplace: Development of a Taxonomy of Adaptive Performance," *Journal of Applied Psychology*, Vol. 85, No. 4, 2000, pp. 612–624.

Pulakos, Elaine D., David W. Dorsey, and Susan S. White, "Understanding Adaptability: A Prerequisite for Effective Performance Within Complex Environments," in C. Shawn Burke, Linda G. Pierce, and Eduardo Salas, eds., *Advances in Human Performance and Cognitive Engineering Research*, Emerald Group Publishing Limited, 2006, pp. 41–71.

Pulakos, Elaine D., Neal Schmitt, David W. Dorsey, Sharon Arad, Jerry W. Hedge, and Walter C. Borman, "Predicting Adaptive Performance: Further Tests of a Model of Adaptability," *Human Performance*, Vol. 15, No. 4, 2002, pp. 299–323.

Randall, Kenneth R., Christian J. Resick, and Leslie A. DeChurch, "Building Team Adaptive Capacity: The Roles of Sensegiving and Team Composition," *Journal of Applied Psychology*, Vol. 96, No. 3, 2011, pp. 525–540.

Ree, Malcolm James, and James A. Earles, "Predicting Training Success: Not Much More Than G," *Personnel Psychology*, Vol. 44, No. 2, 1991, pp. 321–332.

———, "Intelligence Is the Best Predictor of Job Performance," *Current Directions in Psychological Science*, Vol. 1, No. 3, 1992, pp. 86–89. As of August 7, 2014: http://www.jstor.org/stable/20182140

Ree, Malcolm James, James A. Earles, and Mark S. Teachout, "Predicting Job Performance: Not Much More Than G," *Journal of Applied Psychology*, Vol. 79, No. 4, 1994, pp. 518–524.

Ren, Yuqing, Kathleen M. Carley, and Linda Argote, "The Contingent Effects of Transactive Memory: When Is It More Beneficial to Know What Others Know?" *Management Science*, Vol. 52, 2006, pp. 671–682.

Riley, Ryan, Josh Hatfield, A. Paddock, and Jon J. Fallesen, *The 2012 Center for Army Leadership Annual Survey of Leadership (CASAL): Main Findings*, Fort Leavenworth, Kan.: Center for Army Leadership, Technical Report 2013-1, 2013.

Roselle, Holly Sisk, "The Effects of Asymmetric Warfare Adaptability Leadership Program on Adaptability in Soldiers in the U.S. Army," unpublished report, 2013.

Rouiller, Janice Z., and Irwin L. Goldstein, "The Relationship Between Organizational Transfer Climate and Positive Transfer of Training," *Human Resource Development Quarterly*, Vol. 4, No. 4, 1993.

Rulke, Diane L., and Devaki Rau, "Investigating the Encoding Process of Transactive Memory Development in Group Training," *Group and Organization Management*, Vol. 25, 2000, pp. 373–396.

Salas, Eduardo, Deborah DiazGranados, Cameron Klein, C. Shawn Burke, Kevin C. Stagl, Gerald F. Goodwin, and Stanley M. Halpin, "Does Team Training Improve Team Performance? A Meta-Analysis," *Human Factors: The Journal of the Human Factors and Ergonomics Society*, Vol. 50, No. 6, 2008, pp. 903–933.

Salas, Eduardo, Scott I. Tannenbaum, Kurt Kraiger, and Kimberly A. Smith-Jentsch, "The Science of Training and Development in Organizations: What Matters in Practice," *Psychological Science in the Public Interest*, Vol. 13, No. 2, 2012, pp. 74–101.

Savery, John R., and Thomas M. Duffy, *Problem Based Learning: An Instructional Model and Its Constructivist Framework, Constructivist Learning Environments: Case Studies in Instructional Design*, Englewood Cliffs, N.J.: Educational Technology Publications, 1995.

Schmidt, Frank L., and John Hunter, "General Mental Ability in the World of Work: Occupational Attainment and Job Performance," *Journal of Personality and Social Psychology*, Vol. 86, No. 1, 2004, pp. 162–173.

Shanahan, Christopher, Christopher Best, Melandi Finch, and Christopher Sutton, *Measurement of the Behavioural, Cognitive, and Motivational Factors Underlying Team Performance*, Fishermans Bend, Victoria, Australia: DSTO Defence Science and Technology Organization, DSTO-RR-0328, 2007.

Smith, Wally, and John Dowell, "A Case Study of Co-Ordinative Decision-Making in Disaster Management," *Ergonomics*, Vol. 43, 2000, pp. 1153–1166.

Smith-Jentsch, Kimberly A., Joan H. Johnston, and Stephanie C. Payne, "Measuring Team-Related Expertise in Complex Environments," in Janis A. Cannon-Bowers and Eduardo Salas, eds., *Making Decisions Under Stress: Implications for Individual and Team Training*, Washington, D.C.: APA Press, 1998, pp. 61–87.

Steiner, I. D., *Group Process and Productivity*, New York: Academic Press, 1972.

Straus, Susan G., Andrew M. Parker, and James B. Bruce, "The Group Matters: A Review of Processes and Outcomes in Intelligence Analysis," *Group Dynamics: Theory, Research and Practice*, Vol. 15, No. 2, 2011, pp. 128–146.

Straus, Susan G., Michael G. Shanley, Maria C. Lytell, James C. Crowley, Sarah H. Bana, Megan Clifford, and Kristin J. Leuschner, *Enhancing Critical Thinking Skills for Army Leaders Using Blended-Learning Methods*, Santa Monica, Calif.: RAND Corporation, RR-172-A, 2013. As of August 7, 2014: http://www.rand.org/pubs/research_reports/RR172.html

Straus, Susan G., Michael G. Shanley, Douglas Yeung, James Rothenberg, Elizabeth D. Steiner, and Kristin J. Leuschner, *New Tools and Metrics for Evaluating Army Distributed Learning*, Santa Monica, Calif.: RAND Corporation, MG-1072-A, 2011. As of August 7, 2014:
http://www.rand.org/pubs/monographs/MG1072.html

TRADOC—*See* U.S. Army Training and Doctrine Command.

Tucker, Jennifer S., and Katie M. Gunther, "The Application of a Model of Adaptive Performance to Army Leader Behaviors," *Military Psychology*, Vol. 21, 2009, pp. 315–333.

Uitdewilligen, Sjir, Mary J. Waller, and Fred R. H. Zijlstra, "Team Cognition and Adaptability in Dynamic Settings: A Review of Pertinent Work," in Gerald P. Hodgkinson and J. Kevin Ford, eds., *International Review of Industrial and Organizational Psychology*, Chichester, UK: Wiley-Blackwell, 2010.

U.S. Army, "MSAF360: Multi-Source Assessment and Feedback—Overview," website, undated. As of August 11, 2014:
http://msaf.army.mil/Help/Default.aspx

U.S. Army Training and Doctrine Command, *TRADOC Strategic Plan*, undated.

———, "U.S. Army Learning Concept for 2015," TRADOC PAM 525-8-2, January 20, 2011. As of December 20, 2013:
http://www.tradoc.army.mil/tpubs/pams/tp525-8-2.pdf

Walsh, James P., and Liam Fahey, "The Role of Negotiated Belief Structures in Strategy Making," *Journal of Management*, Vol. 12, 1986, pp. 325–338.

Watkins, K. E., H. A. Pincus, Susan Paddock, Brad Smith, Abigail Woodroffe, Carrie Farmer, Melanie E. Sorbero, Marcela Horvitz-Lennon, Thomas Mannle, Kimberly A. Hepner, Jacob Solomon, and Cathy Call, "Care for Veterans with Mental and Substance Use Disorders: Good Performance but Room to Improve on Many Measures," *Health Affairs*, Vol. 30, No. 11, 2011, pp. 2194–203.

Weick, Karl E., "The Vulnerable System: An Analysis of the Tenerife Air Disaster," *Journal of Management*, Vol. 16, 1990, pp. 571–593.

———, "The Collapse of Sensemaking in Organizations: The Mann Gulch Disaster," *Administrative Science Quarterly*, Vol. 38, No. 4, 1993, pp. 628–652.

White, Susan S., Rose A. Mueller-Hanson, David W. Dorsey, Elaine D. Pulakos, Michelle M. Wisecarver, Edwin A. Deagle III, and Kip G. Mendini, *Developing Adaptive Proficiency in Special Forces Officers*, Arlington, Va.: U.S. Army Research Institute for the Behavioral and Social Sciences, Research Report 1831, February 2005.

Wildman, Jessica L., Wendy L. Bedwell, Eduardo Salas, and Kimberly A. Smith-Jentsch, "Performance Measurement at Work: A Multilevel Perspective," in Sheldon Zedeck, ed., *APA Handbook of Industrial and Organizational Psychology*, Washington, D.C.: American Psychological Association, 2011, pp. 303–341.

Wonderlic, Inc., *Wonderlic Contemporary Cognitive Ability Test (WPT-R) Administrator's Guide*, Vernon Hills, Ill.: Wonderlic, Inc., 2012.

Zaccaro, Stephen J., "Trait-Based Perspectives of Leadership," *American Psychologist*, Vol. 62, No. 1, 2007, pp. 6–16.

Zaccaro, Stephen J., Deanna Banks, Lee Kiechel-Koles, Cary Kemp, and Paige Bader, *Leader and Team Adaptation: The Influence and Development of Key Attributes and Processes*, Arlington, Va.: U.S. Army Research Institute for the Behavioral and Social Sciences, Technical Report 1256, August 2009.